The Camp Scott Murders

C.S. Kelly

ISBN-10: 150015735X
ISBN-13: 978-1500157357

1st edition

DEDICATION

To
three little girls who tragically lost their lives

Lori Lee Farmer,

Michele Heather Guse,

And

Doris Denise Milner

Thanks
to
My Family and Friends

Special Thanks
to
Kevin and all your help
Plus
Holly and Jane for your editing

CONTENTS

ACKNOWLEDGMENTS

This research should be used as a resource of information given about the 37 years following the murders.

It was never the author's intent to put together the following information for anyone except as a personal research resource of evidence.

Research on the available data and placing into a timeline of events, without emphases on one suspect or from one point of view became the author's goal.

The purpose was to take all ideas and come up with a timeline that would follow from June 1977 to the present day, in a facts-at-a-glance resource guide of the events as they unfolded.

This **IS NOT** to take the place of the books and online resources providing a greater, in-depth, look at the people and places involved throughout the years. This is a research resource that should be used in <u>combination</u> with the current books and online resources.

Best book on Gene Hart:
"Tent Number Eight", by Gloyd McCoy

Best Online resources:
www.girlscoutmurders.com
www.campscottmurders.com
girlscoutmurders.yuku.com

3 Girl Scouts Murdered in Camp

1

MURDER

Locust Grove, Oklahoma 1977. The Girl Scout murders were the most bizarre crimes in the history of Oklahoma. Three little girls murdered less than 24 hours after arriving at Camp Scott.

Murdered in the night, without a sound, only a few hundred yards from their counselors' tent and only a few yards from 7 other tents filled with 28 campers, 4 girls to a tent within the Kiowa Encampment. In total 140 girls had arrived at Camp Scott on June 12th, 1977 and three young girls would become the target of a violent and heinous crime.

During the night, someone or several individuals came through the back of a tent where the three girls were sleeping. All three were hit in the head with a blunt object, possibly killing two of the girls instantly, but the third would be bound, gagged and made to walk to the edge of the camp road, where she was raped and strangled to death.

Doris Denis Milner was left on top of her sleeping bag, mostly nude, with the other two girls, zipped up in their sleeping bags and left beside her in a pile, 150 yards from their tent. When discovered, scores of lawmen including the Sheriff department, Highway patrol, FBI, The Oklahoma State Bureau of Investigation (OSBI) arrived. Throughout the next few days tracking dogs, helicopters with infrared sensors, and hundreds of private citizens joined in what would become the largest manhunt in Oklahoma state history.

Through the next 36 years, many events would happen; hopes of finding the killer or killers; people claiming to know who did the crimes; lawsuits; speculations; newspaper articles; DNA tests;

websites; online forums; videos; TV documentaries; books; and even talks of movies. But in the end, it remained a homicide cold case that shook the nation, to the core, in 1977.

Before the nightmare, Camp Scott had accommodated as many as 800 girls each summer, but now, the campfire stories of a boogie man, lurking in the woods, became real!

2

DETAILS OF THE CASE
REPORTED 1977 TO THE PRESENT DAY

Three Girl Scouts Killed
After Assaults in Camp

June 12th, 1977 – Approximately 140 girls of all ages arrive at
Camp Scott located in Locust Grove, Oklahoma, for a 2 week
summer camp. Heavy rains prevailed in the evening, finally
stopping as all the girls settled in for the 1st night.

June 13th, 1977 – Just after 6am Kiowa Camp Counselor Carla
Wilhite headed for a shower and noticed sleeping bags beside the
camp road, and then she saw the body of Denise Milner. Zipped
in two other sleeping bags were the bodies of Lori Farmer and
Michele Guse. Doris Denise Milner, 10 and Lori Lee Farmer, 8,
both of Tulsa, and Michele Guse, 9, of Broken Arrow had been
bludgeoned, repeatedly assaulted and taken 150 yards away from
their tent to a camp road where their bodies were found.

Evidence found at the camp included a red 6v flashlight, partial roll of black electrical tape, rope, a pair of glasses, and bloody shoe and boot tracks inside their tent.

The bodies

The sleeping bags

June 13th, 1977 – The camp was closed immediately and the campers, unaware of what had happened, were brought back from Camp Scott in Chartered buses to the Scouting Council headquarters in Tulsa, Oklahoma.[1]

June 14th, 1977 – The day after the murders, the mother of a nine year old girl, Nancy, who had been attending Camp Scott, gave accounts of how waiting to know if her daughter was all right was horrible. On Monday morning, June 13th, Mrs. Kitzmiller heard over the car radio that 3 girls had been slain at Camp Scott. Not knowing if it was her daughter who was murdered, Mrs. Kitzmiller and her husband started driving toward Camp Scott located in Locust Grove and passed the chartered buses, heading back to the Tulsa Girl Scout, Magic Empire Council headquarters. They turned their car around and headed back where they met up with their daughter Nancy and took her home.

As the disappointed campers filed off the buses and were reunited with their terrified parents, the campers had no idea what had just happened at Camp Scott.[2]

June 14th, 1977 – The entire town of Locust Grove, Oklahoma, was frightened and in shock after the killings. Parents were now afraid to let kids camp out, and neighbors were afraid to leave their houses.[3]

Screams awaken girl, then camp was silent

June 14th, 1977 – It was reported that on the first night at camp, Wilma Tenant of Stillwater, a camper at Camp Scott, was awakened in the night by nearby screams; Wilma told a counselor who discounted the disturbance and told her to go back to sleep. [4]

June 14th, 1977 - The wooden floor of the murdered girls' tent was removed for examination, it's covered with blood. No murder weapon had been found and it's revealed that a tennis shoe and boot print are found inside and outside the tent.[5]

Search Dogs Roam Slaying Site

June 15th, 1977 – Team of three, specially trained, tracking dogs were flown in from Pennsylvania and were volunteered to help in the manhunt. Two German shepherds named 'Harras' and 'Dutch' and one German Rottweiler named 'Butz', the dogs would help establish the entrance and exit of the killer at the camp.[6]

2 of the 3 tracking dogs

June 15th, 1977 - Sheriff Weaver mentioned Gene Hart as a possible suspect. OSBA agents revealed they had found footprints, fingerprints, a flashlight, tape, and a piece of electrical cord as evidence.[7]

June 15th, 1977 – The Magic Empire Council of Girl Scouts started a $1000 reward fund with donations made by its board of directors and the Fourth National Bank of Tulsa.[8]

June 15th, 1977 – Throughout Oklahoma, Security was increased at Camps. A Group of Campfire Girls left Tulsa, Oklahoma, June 14th, 1977 to begin their summer camp sessions and were accompanied by armed guards.[9]

June 16th, 1977 – Three of the Girl Scout Counselors were questioned. The eyeglasses and glasses case owned by one of the counselors was found along the killer's path. Officials revealed the killer had walked by the counselors' tent to get to the site where the three bodies were found.[10]

Also, it's revealed by authorities, that a blue denim purse was stolen from the counselor's tent in the Kiowa unit at Camp Scott the night of the murders.[11]

June 16th, 1977 – Camp Garland, the Boy Scout camp, 3 miles across the road from Camp Scott remained open. Of the 130 boys at the camp, only 13 parents had picked up their sons on Monday, June 13th. Some additional security measures were added, but the camp was never closed.[12]

Map of Camps location to each other

June 16th, 1977 – Three fingerprints and several footprints were reportedly found, Officials had theorized the killer burglarized the counselors tent and had also broken into a nearby unnamed farmhouse. Although all three girls had been sexually molested, possibly by an unidentified object, District Attorney Sid Wise believed the slayings were not the work of a "woman homosexual".[13]

June 17th, 1977 – Sid Wise, District Attorney, took News reporters on a tour of the roped off murder site at Camp Scott. Reporters had been kept outside the camp since the slayings. Wise pointed at the tree near Kiowa's camp where the bodies had been found. Official investigators continued to weave through the trees and thick bush with metal detectors looking for additional evidence. Wise indicated he was puzzled how the crime was committed without awakening anyone. Meanwhile, authorities had removed pieces of the victims' tent canvas and the wooden floor, soaked with blood, and had areas cut away and sent off for analyses.[14]

June 17th, 1977 – Special telephone hotline was set up and authorities hoped the killer would call and confess to the slayings. Sid Wise, the District Attorney said "Sometimes people with deranged minds want to be caught". [15]

June 18th, 1977 - Two of the three tracking dogs from Pennsylvania, died. The Rottweiler named 'Butz' died from heat stroke, and the German Sheppard named 'Harras' was struck by an automobile and killed while being returned to his home in Pennsylvania.[16]

June 19th, 1977 – It's finally revealed that the 110 acre ranch located less than a mile west of Camp Scott appeared to have been burglarized during the time of the murders. The killer had possibly been at the ranch prior to the slayings. Investigators had found a footprint and several fingerprints on the property. The tape, used to bind one of the victims, matched tape missing from the ranch house. At a pond on the property, ashes from a recent campfire were discovered. The owner, Jack Shroff, who was away at the time of the murders, took and passed a lie detector test given to him by the Oklahoma State Bureau of Investigation and his alibi was also confirmed.[17]

June 19th, 1977 – Barbara Day, the director at Camp Scott, was upset that a "sick society" would prevent Camp Scott from ever being the same again; the effects would be felt worldwide. She didn't know how to respond to her 9 year old daughter who wanted to know if they would ever go back to Camp Scott.[18]

June 21st, 1977 – Oklahoma Governor, David Boren, offered the support of the National Guard; Mayes County Sheriff Weaver refused the help because he felt his men were sufficient.[19]

June 22nd, 1977– Frederick Daily Leader newspaper reported that five boy scouts at Camp Garland had been questioned by the OSBI about their contact, in May, with a teenage camper who said he was from Tulsa, Oklahoma. Described as pale and skinny teenager, he ate with the boy scouts then stole a hatchet, hunting knife and whetstone from them.[20]

June 22nd, 1977 – Two photographs of three women were found in a cave two miles from the murder scene. The pictures showed up in newspapers where they would end up being identified.[7]

June 23rd, 1977 – Gene Hart, a convicted rapist on the run since escaping in 1973 from the Mayes County Jail at Pryor, Oklahoma, was officially charged with the slayings, just 10 days after the murders occurred. The Manhunt for Hart began. Officials disclosed that the photos found in the cave, of three women, were developed and printed by Hart, who was serving time at Granite Reformatory in Eastern Oklahoma from 1967 to 1969 and had worked in the darkroom for a former prison photographer who had free-lance and taken the pictures at a wedding in 1968.[21]

June 23rd, 1977 – A farm owner saw a man sitting in a cave just two miles west of Camp Scott. The farmer was walking his fence line saw the man sitting under a cliff on the other side of his fence, just 10 feet away. When he got back to his house he called the police. When law enforcement arrived the man was already gone.[22]

Search Party Begins Hunt

June 24th, 1977 – Richard Guse, father of Michelle Guse, joined the volunteers who searched the camp area for the killer. Hundreds of law officers and volunteers joined the hunt. Guse indicated he didn't want others to do all the work; he wanted to help find the person who had killed his daughter.[23]

Sheriff Pete Weaver organizing search

June 26th, 1977 – The search of 6 square miles of hilly, wooded and brush covered area, known as Skunk Mountain, just a mile from Camp Scott had turned up possible new evidence, but authorities refused to comment.

Items picked up during the search, were placed in white plastic bags for analysis by crime lab technicians. They included two men's jackets, a pair of blue jeans, a T shirt with rust colored stains, several empty soft drink cans and some empty egg cartons.[24]

June 28th, 1977 – The hunt for the accused killer had authorities using the latest in technology, three heat sensing devices attached to National Guard helicopters. Pilots flew grid patterns over the

15

area around Camp Scott and kept in radio contact with five Special Weapons and Tactics (SWAT) teams on the ground. District Attorney Sid Wise, leader of the investigation, felt the killer eluded detection because of numerous caves in the region, more than authorities even knew existed.[25]

July 1st, 1977 – Since June 13th, lawmen had operated the investigation into the murders from one of Camp Scott's buildings and now were leaving the camp. The Patrol mobile command post vehicle was moved back to Oklahoma City. The Highway Patrol troopers and a nine man tactical squadron were also sent home.[26]

July 9th, 1977 – Magic Empire Council of Girl Scouts announced summer camp would reopen, *for day camp only*, at an undisclosed location. Council estimated 800 girls were to have spent the summer of 77 at Camp Scott.[27]

July 11th, 1977 – Dr. Robert R. Phillips drew a personality profile of the killer for a group of Associated Press affiliates. He felt the killer of the girls at Camp Scott was a sadistic psychopath with sexual perversions who might repeat the heinous crime if not captured. Mentally, the killer could not tolerate the idea of rejection and his rage overwhelmed him. The murderer was not feeble minded, knew right from wrong, and did not act on impulse. Dr. Philips took his personality sketch from newspaper articles describing the murder scene. He deducted that the killer was cool, calculated and probably kept the camp under surveillance before he moved in. He came prepared with a flashlight, blunt instrument and tape, and was in complete control until he became caught up which caused him to become careless. The killer tried to bring order to the chaos by a futile attempt to wipe up the blood in the tent. Something happened, and he was frightened away, leaving behind his flashlight and other objects.[28]

July 13th, 1977 – One month after the murders, The Midweek, a feature magazine of the Tulsa Tribune reported: "A crime that called for no-holds-barred investigation, regardless of expense, sleepless nights and long hours". More than 200 lawmen, 400 volunteers, loaned expensive heat sensing devices, reward funds, and at that point 30 days after the murders, the investigation continued with questions that remained unanswered and evidence had remained a mystery.[29]

Victims Shoes Add Strange New Twist In Scout Killings

July 29th, 1977 – Reported by the Tulsa Tribune, a pair of tennis shoes, with the handwritten name of Denise Milner, was found on the steps of the building used as the command post at Camp Scott.[30]

NOTE: See details in the section "Troubling events after June 1977"

September 22nd, 1977 – The parents of 2 of the murdered Girl Scouts filed a 3 million dollar lawsuit against Camp Scott's Magic Empire Council.[31]

September 23rd, 1977 – Wade Farman, reportedly donated two St. Bernard's as attack dogs to help patrol Camp Scott and provide security for camp once guards were removed.[32]

March 10th, 1978 – A man, whom officers had said bore an uncanny resemblance to Gene Hart, was released after his fingerprints did not match Hart's. The man was arrested in Springfield, Missouri and had matched all physical and occupational descriptions of Hart.[33]

April 6th, 1978 – Gene Leroy Hart was captured. After 10 months on the run, during which Hart eluded one of the largest manhunts in Oklahoma history. State investigators found Hart living in a remote cabin. They captured him at the small backwoods shack in the Cookson Hills of Cherokee County, 50 miles from where the murders happened. Apprehended at the home of an elderly man, Sam Pigeon Jr., Hart was taken to Tahlequah and fingerprinted, then transferred to the state penitentiary at McAlester, Oklahoma, where he had been serving a prison term of 1st degree rape prior to escape from Mayes County Jail in 1973.[34]

April 11th, 1978 – Hart pleaded innocent to the triple killings. Charges had been filed against him just 10 days after the murders.

He was brought to the Locust Grove, Oklahoma Courthouse where he was charged with three counts of 1st degree murder; District Judge William Whistler decreed all three murder cases consolidated, and the preliminary trial would start in June. Outside the Courthouse approximately 300 spectators congregated.[35]

June 7th, 1978 – The first day of the preliminary hearing of the Girl Scout murder charges against Gene Leroy Hart began. Evidence collected, for almost a year, became public during the hearings, which lasted from June 7th to July 6th, 1978.[36]

Note: Parts of the pretrial transcript can be viewed at the website: girlscoutmurders.com

Carla Wilhite, Camp counselor at the Kiowa encampment, testified she had found the murdered girls along the camps path on her way to the showers at 6am on June 13th. She was asked about any unusual things happening during the week, before the scouts arrived. She related a story of hearing footsteps and a strange scratching sound on the screen door, late one night, at the camp staff house. When asked if there were any homosexuals at the camp, she replied she didn't know of any. Another camp counselor at the Kiowa encampment, Dee Ann Elder testified that one of the Kiowa tents had a slash in the flap sometime right before the scouts arrived.[37]

June 8th, 1978 – During the preliminary trial, Camp counselor Dee Ann Elder testified that on the morning of June 13th, she had run to the end tent in the seven tent encampment to begin a tent check after counselor, Carla Wilhite, told her to count the kids. She opened the tent flap and found no children, no sleeping bags and no mattress covers on the mattresses. All she saw was blood on the mattresses and blood on the tent floor. [38]

June 9th, 1978 – During the Preliminary trial, it was revealed that a note that warned of murders at Camp Scott had been found several weeks before the killings. Barbara Day, Director of Camp Scott, testified that the note had been found in April 1977 by Michelle Hoffman, a senior Girl Scout attending the camp. The threat had been considered a prank and not brought to anyone's attention until later in the summer. The exact words of the note were not available because the note had been destroyed soon after it was discovered.[39]

Barbara Day also recounted that, on June 13th at 6am, camp counselor Dee Ann Elder came to the Director's office and alerted them to the situation. Barbara and her husband Richard rushed to where the bodies were; one of the slain girls lay on top of a sleeping bag with no clothes from the waist down and dried blood from a head wound. Nearby were 2 other sleeping bags with the other 2 girls' bodies inside them. Richard Day voiced his concerns on not touching anything, while someone else suggested covering the exposed body, Richard Day covered the body without disturbing or moving it. Ben Woodward, the camp ranger testified that he found a roll of tape and a flashlight with the lens covered with a piece of green plastic except for a tiny hole to allow a narrow beam of light.[40]

June 11th, 1978 – Larry Mullins, fingerprint technician for the Oklahoma State Bureau of Investigations, testified that two fingerprints were found and taken from the flashlight found near the bodies and from a cot in the slain girls' tent. He had disassembled the flashlight and found a newspaper clipping stuffed between the battery and bottom of the flashlight. A piece of green plastic with a small hole had been taped over the lens which would only allow a small beam of light to be emitted. No fingerprints had been found on the plastic case of the flashlight or battery, but there was a latent fingerprint on the reflector inside the flashlight. No identification had been made from the fingerprints he had found on the flashlight or the cot.

Other Testimony showed the intruder, who killed the girls, had been prepared. Introduced into evidence was tape and cord that had been used to bind two of the girls and additional cord and cloth that had been used on the third child.[41]

June 12th, 1978 - During the Preliminary trial hearing, Dr. Neal Hoffman, medical examiner, testified that the girls probably died between 4 and 6am. One was strangled and the other two died from blows to the head.[42]

June 24th, 1978 – Security had been stepped up at camps after the murders in 1977. Security, now a bigger concern, caused precautions to be taken nationwide which would include large floodlights, more men present at camps, extra night watchmen, patrol dogs and locked gates. Some camps started requiring counselors to sleep in the tents with the campers, while other camps increased the ratio from twelve campers per each adult to six campers per each adult.[43]

June 27th, 1978 – At the preliminary hearing, additional information was shared including unknown men being seen at Camp Scott, days prior to the slayings. Two counselors had been frightened by two men at the camp, the night before the murders. Celia Stall, unit leader at Camp Scott, told of how campers had voiced concerns of seeing a man behind their tent wearing khaki clothes and army boots, whereas another man was seen by a latrine the night of the murders.[44]

In two incidents during the week before camp began, Miss Stall testified that two staff members were followed by someone with a flashlight. In another incident, her friend had seen a man enter her tent.[45]

Richard Day, husband of the camp Director Barbara Day, testified he had encountered a stranger in the camp, the day before the scouts arrived, wearing jeans and a work shirt, carrying a clear plastic jug, and looking for water.[46]

June 28th, 1978 – In the preliminary hearing to determine if the state had enough evidence to hold Gene Hart for trial, it was revealed that two separate bloody foot tracks were found inside the tent. One track appeared to be of a military type boot and the other had been left by a type of tennis shoe.[47]

A similar military type print was found on the trail between two of the camp units, and a similar boot print was found behind a nearby home, which was adjacent to Camp Scott. The house had been burglarized and items taken, which included a two inch roll of black duct tape and nylon rope, similar to the roll of tape found near the bodies and rope which was used to bind one of the girls.[48]

June 30th, 1978 – Three caves south of Locust Grove near Camp Scott appeared to be related to the murders. The first Cave, located at Spring Creek, was about three miles from the camp and was discovered by squirrel hunters four days after the murders. Authorities found evidence, including sunglasses, green plastic and masking tape, similar to the tape on the flashlight found near the girls' bodies. Part of a newspaper matching the newspaper inside the battery compartment of the flashlight near the bodies was also discovered in the cave. Also, the two wedding photographs, which Hart had apparently developed in 1968, were found there.

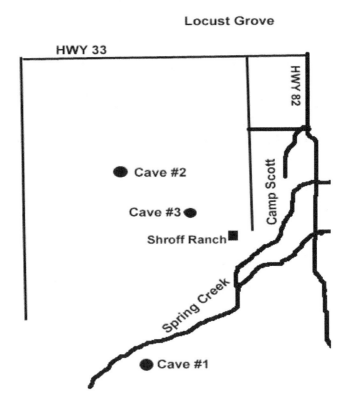

Approximate Cave Location

Cave #2, a ledge along Skunk Mountain and about two miles from the camp, authorities discovered a boot print, which matched the boot print found in the murdered girls' tent and also matched a boot print found outside Shroff's Ranch. Yet another boot print was identified outside a grocery store at Sam's Corner that had been burglarized shortly after the murders and appeared to be linked to the killings. A cigarette butt taken from cave #2 was tested for saliva and was determined to be Type O blood. Authorities linked a Vienna sausage can found at a pond near cave #2 as one from the burglarized grocery at Sam's Corner.

Taunting Message 'Killer Was Here' Scrawled on Cave Walls

Cave #3, a mile from Camp Scott, and located on Jack Shroff's property, was where officials found a message written on the wall of the cave that read: "The killer was here. Bye Bye Fools. 77-6-17."

A young prison inmate had led authorities to the cave in late July 1977.[49]

July 7th, 1978 – At the close of the preliminary trial, Gene Hart was ordered by Special District Judge Jess B. Clanton, to stand trial for first-degree murders of the 3 girls. There was probable cause to believe he had committed the crimes.[50]

November 24th, 1978 – It's revealed that Mayes County District Attorney, Sid Wise, had signed an agreement with a Pryor newsman, Ron Grimsley, to coauthor a book about the Girl Scout murders just four months after the June 1977 murders. Wise had allowed Grimsley to view secret OSBI and FBI investigative reports about the crimes, and Wise was to receive 75 percent of the proceeds from the book sales. After details of the arrangement were disclosed, Sid Wise bowed out of his involvement in the case. Any prosecution would be led by Tulsa County District Attorney S. M. Fallis Jr., Fallis had assisted in the case since June 1978 when he was asked to join the team on the eve of the preliminary hearing for Gene Hart.[51]

March 5th, 1979 – Jury selection began for the first degree murder trial of Gene Leroy Hart. This selection would take from March 5th until the trial began on March 19th, 1979.

March 19th, 1979 – The first day of trial began for the Murder charges against Gene Hart. The jury consisted of 6 men and 6 women. The courthouse was packed and included the parents of the murdered girls, who attended every day of the trial.[52]

March 20, 1979 –Camp counselor Dee Ann Elder was the first witness to testify during the trial. She testified that at about 10:30pm on June 12th, she saw the three girls in their tent laying in their beds, chatting happily, and one was reading a book, only hours before the slayings happened. The next morning after the initial find of the slain bodies, the Kiowa counselors began going to each tent and counting the kids.[53]

March 22, 1979 – During the trial, photographs of the murder scene and photographic slides of the victims' mutilated bodies were viewed by the jurors. Certain photos were eliminated due to the graphic content that could have been too overwhelming for the jury to view.

Dr. Neal Hoffman, Tulsa County medical examiner, told the jury that all 3 girls had been beaten, possibly by the head of a camp ax. The Milner girl died of strangulation, and the other two girls were killed by blows to the head with a blunt object. He also described the condition of the bound and mutilated bodies and told how all three were sexually assaulted; however he believed one girl was sexually assaulted after her death, due to the lack of bleeding from her wounds.[54]

March 23rd, 1979 – Ann Reed, OSBI technician, testified that microscopic examination of hair found on Milner's body and in the victims' tent, and hair samples taken from Hart showed identical characteristics.[55]

March 27th, 1979 – Two chemists, one a former Oklahoma State Health Department chemist, testified: hair and other samples taken from Gene Hart failed to positively link him to the deaths. Hair samples were similar but nothing more. They could only give possible clues to someone's race, but could not point to a particular person. Hart and the victims shared the same blood type.[56]

March 29th, 1979 – The last witness called to testify was Mrs. Dean Boyd, who worked in a Cafe in Chouteau, Oklahoma, just 15 miles from Camp Scott. She testified that on June 13th between 5am and 6am, a man came into the Café acting nervously. He kept looking down at his shoes and talked about having car trouble. Mrs. Boyd did not identify him as looking like Gene Hart but indicated he looked more like William "Bill" Stevens from a picture she saw of Stevens two years after the unidentified man had been in the café. Authorities had already taken hair, blood and sperm samples from Stevens, who was imprisoned in Kansas for an unrelated crime. The samples were analyzed and eliminated him as a suspect.[57]

March 30th, 1979 - Hart was acquitted after a month long trial in the slayings. The six men, six woman jury, said Hart was innocent of entering the tent, bludgeoning the three girls and repeatedly assaulting them. The verdict stunned the parents of the slain girls while Gene Hart's family began to rejoice, and Hart himself began to sob. The verdict left the major question of who was guilty.

The investigation into the Girl Scout Murders was not renewed, despite the jury's decision that Hart was proved innocent of the crimes.[58]

Note: To learn more details about the Gene Hart trial please read, "Tent Number Eight" by Gloyd McCoy.

March 31st, 1979 – Gene Hart was returned to the state penitentiary prison in McAlester, Oklahoma, where he still owed the state on a 308 year prison term for other unrelated crimes he had committed.[59]

April 19th, 1979 – Newspaper reported, William "Bill" Alton Stevens, had denied involvement in the Girl Scout murders. On January 3rd, OSBI agents had interviewed Dewayne Peters at a Kansas prison where both Peters and Stevens were serving life sentences for rape, robbery and kidnapping of a Garden City schoolteacher. Stevens said he was unfamiliar with Camp Scott area and had worked on a Seminole construction site no where near Locust Grove, the morning that the bodies were found.[60]

May 16th, 1979 – The families of two of the slain Girl Scouts sued for $3.5 million. This amended the September 1977 lawsuit petition and added $500,000 in damages for physical pain, mental shock, horror and anguish suffered by Doris Milner. The petition had also asked to add The Girl Scouts Magic Empire Council's insurance providers, Hartford accident & Indemnity Company,

Hartford Casualty Insurance Company and the Hartford Fire Insurance Company.[61]

June 1st, 1979 – Gene Hart gave an exclusive interview with the Cherokee Advocate three days before dying of a heart attack in prison.

Gene Hart and both of his attorneys, Garvin Isaacs and Gary Pitchlynn, were present when the interview was conducted.[62]

June 4th, 1979 - Hart died at age 35 of an apparent heart attack at the Oklahoma State Penitentiary in McAlester, Oklahoma, where he was serving a 308-year sentence on convictions unrelated to the Camp Scott killings. Hart maintained his innocence until his death. An autopsy was performed by Dr. Fred Jordan, the medical examiner who confirmed that Hart suffered from heart disease. Several days later, more than a thousand people attended his funeral at the Locust Grove High School Gym.[63]

June 12th, 1979 – A nude man was chased from a Girl Scout tent in Topeka, Kansas. The camp counselor at Camp Daisy Hindman was awakened by a noise around midnight, and discovered a man wearing only shoes in a tent where four girls were sleeping. The counselor chased the man out of the tent and caught him; however, the man struck her in the head with a flashlight and got away. Police were called in but did not apprehend the man. The man was described as 20 to 25 years old, five feet eleven, long blonde hair tied in a ponytail, with a red and white skull and crossbones tattoo on chest.[64]

1981 – "Someone Cry For the Children" The 1st Book Published about the murders was announced, written by Dick Wilkerson, former deputy director of the Oklahoma State Crime Bureau and his brother Mike Wilkerson, who was the agent in charge of the investigation.[65]

1981 - The Tulsa-based, Girl Scouts Magic Empire Council acquired land on the Jack Zink Ranch in Osage County and formed Camp Tallchief. No traditional summer camp had occurred since the time of the murders in 1977. At Camp Tallchief, the scouts would sleep in raised cabins rather than in tents, and the camp would have fewer trees, which were said to have aided the killer at Camp Scott. Security measures also were heightened for the new location. Security at Tallchief included a large fence surrounding the camp with barbed wire along the top.[66]

June 13th, 1982 – The Future of Camp Scott, which had never been reopened since the murders, was in doubt; no decision had been made by the Girl Scout Magic Empire Council. The gate stayed locked, and posted signs warned that the area was guarded by camp ranger R.A. Martin. The former camp ranger, who had been there at the time of the slayings, had moved to Kansas in the years following the tragedy.[67]

May 12ᵗʰ, 1984 - Mayes County Sheriff Paul Smith announced he knew who had raped and murdered the three girls, and it wasn't Gene Hart. His three suspects were all natives of Locust Grove. Smith had a roofing hammer he felt was the possible murder weapon, and he was having it tested in a police laboratory. He also had divers searching Fort Gibson Reservoir for a car that he believed the suspects were driving the day of the killings. Sheriff Smith felt more than one person was responsible in the slayings, because two different types of weapons were used to bludgeon the girls, possibly a tool with a hammer head and also a blunt instrument such as a wrench or pipe. Also, the children were bound with two different types of knots, a single loop knot and a double half hitch knot indicating, again, that two or more people were involved in the slayings.

Smith had succeeded Mayes County Sheriff Weaver in the 1980 sheriff's race. Weaver maintained he felt Smith was using the Girl Scout case as a way to get reelected, as sheriff, in future elections. Weaver was haunted by the murders and had trouble forgetting the crime scene, which he had seen the morning of the murders. Weaver was "1,000 percent" convinced it was Gene Hart who had killed the girls or he, himself, would still be out there looking for the killer.[68]

May 16ᵗʰ, 1984– OSBI discounted Sheriff Paul Smith's claims. Tests conducted on the hammer at the OSBI laboratory showed the hammer design did not match the pattern on the weapon that had caused the injuries to the girls, and the divers did not locate a car in Fort Gibson Reservoir. The woman who was a key witness admitted lying to Sheriff Smith.[69]

June 1984 - Charles and Sheri Farmer, parents of Lori Farmer, organized the Oklahoma chapter of Parents of Murdered Children, honoring, what would have been Lori's 16th Birthday on June 18th. Sheri Farmer felt there should be priority on getting information to victims' families regarding their rights, because of how difficult it was for her to get information and know her rights about what had happened to Lori.[70]

June 13th, 1984 - Mayes County Sheriff, Paul Smith, still wanted to pursue the Girl Scout Murders, even though no new charges had been considered by the OSBI after reviewing Smith's 250-page investigative report on the murders. Previously in May, Smith had announced he had three prime suspects and a roofing hammer he thought was the murder weapon, and had divers searching Fort Gibson Reservoir. The OSBI, in response, launched an active investigation of the case which had ended.[71]

July 14th, 1984 – William "Bill" A. Stevens dies in prison at age 27; he was stabbed to death in his cell at the Kansas State Penitentiary in Lansing. Stevens, at age 22, had been a possible suspect and became a key figure in the 1979 trial of Gene Leroy Hart for the Girl Scout murders. Stevens had been eliminated by the OSBI as a suspect before the trial of Hart.

Mrs. Dean Boyd, a waitress in Chouteau just 12 miles from Camp Scott, claimed he was the one she saw coming into the café the morning of July 13th, 1977. The man kept looking down at his hands and boots. She had called authorities after he left.[72]

March 18th, 1985 – The Civil Suit trial began in Tulsa County District Court, in which the parents, Dr. Charles and Sherri Farmer and Walter and Bettye Milner, had filed for damages from the Magic Empire Council of Girl Scouts, and Hartford Insurance Co., which insured Camp Scott.

The parents believed the negligence of the scout council and insurance company allowed their daughters' deaths. Each family sued for $3.5 million in actual and punitive damages.[73]

March 27th, 1985 - By a 9-3 vote, jurors found in favor of the Magic Empire Council and the Hartford Accident and Indemnity Co. in the lawsuit.[74]

Note: Read about the Civil Lawsuit in the section "Parents' Lawsuit goes to Trial"

March 29th, 1985 – The day after a Tulsa County Jury ruled in favor of the Girl Scouts Magic Empire Council, Mayes County

Sheriff H.W. "Chief" Jordan announced that he was working on a small lead in the case. Several individuals merited checking into by Jordan, who had taken over as the Mayes County Sheriff two months prior, but he was not sure if Paul Smith had already followed up on the same leads.[75]

June 6th, 1985 - The parents filed an appeal to the Oklahoma Supreme Court after jury's refusal to award damages for the deaths.[76]

December 16th, 1986 - The State Court of Appeals upheld the 1985 decision that the Magic Empire of Girl Scouts and its insurance company were not liable for the murders.[77]

August 1988 – Camp Scott, Bonnie Brewster, Director of the Magic Empire Council of the Girl Scouts announced Camp Scott was for sale. Camp Scott, owned by the Tulsa-based council since 1928, had not been open since the June 1977 murders. Several acres on the south end of the former camp site were sold in spring 1987. The remaining land was sold in late 1988.[78]

1989 – Charles Sasser's book, "The Girl Scout Murders" published by Delacorte Press, was pulled from its shipping schedule. The book, a factual account of the murders, was written but never released due to possible copyright infringements because of its similarity to the Wilkerson book "Someone Cry for the Children".[79]

July 7th, 1989 – First DNA evidence was delivered to the FBI to evaluate and perform tests. The DNA testing was called DNA fingerprinting and the FBI made a special exception in the case of the Girl Scout killings, breaking a rule that it accepts only active cases. At the time, this technique took a maximum of eight weeks, allowing the isolation of DNA from body fluids such as blood, semen and saliva. DNA was chemically extracted from stained materials. Once obtained, the DNA was cut into small fragments with DNA probes. No two people have the same DNA, with the exception of identical twins.[80]

October 24th, 1989 – The first DNA tests failed to conclusively answer questions that could have solved the murders.[81]

October 25th, 1989 - Genetic testing conducted by the FBI linked Gene Leroy Hart to the slayings, but could not determine conclusively whether he was the killer. Hart's body fluids matched 3 out of 5 probes of DNA evidence obtained at the crime scene, and two other tests were inconclusive. Reported evidence forwarded to the FBI included a pillowcase stained with seminal fluid as well as a known blood sample from Hart. OSBI officials asked the FBI to conduct the tests because the samples were old, but the federal lab had little experience handling such old and deteriorating evidence, and so the results were inconclusive.[82]

August 20th, 1990 – Minister, Rev. Gerald Manley, claimed to have seen the killings, and that he could identify two of the killers. Manley claimed he ran out of gas, late one night, and two young men drove up to help him. The men were discussing a purse stolen from a counselor's tent at Camp Scott. After the Minister got gas and left the men, it was late, so he pulled his car over and went to sleep. Manley claimed one of the men woke him up and brought him to a tent in the Girl Scout camp. Two unknown men were standing outside the tent; he did not recognize the men. In the tent, Manley claimed he had seen one of the girls on the floor, and two others zipped-up in sleeping bags. OSBI later said the minister had brought the story forward, years ago, and had nothing to substantiate the claim.[83]

November 1990 – Oklahoma Television Channel 2 KTEW/KJRH and Sportscaster/Newsman anchor Jerry Webber produced a week-long segment called "The Girl Scout Murders Case," that ran on Channel 2. Some felt Mr. Webber shed no new light on the murders.[84]

October 11th, 1991 - Former Mayes County Sheriff Glen "Pete" Weaver died at the age of 71. The Mayes County sheriff had received national attention during the Girl Scout murders in 1977.

In 1987, stress from the murders had caused him to have two heart attacks. Weaver believed Gene Hart was the killer until the day he died.[85]

Slayings Probe Continues

March 23rd, 1993 – Lawsuit seeks items claimed as Girl Scout slaying link. Ted LaTurner wanted the Oklahoma State Bureau of Investigation to return the items he believed to be key in solving the Girl Scout Murders. LaTurner filed a lawsuit in Mayes County District Court seeking the return of items state agents had allegedly confiscated from him in 1989 and 1990. LaTurner said the items had some bearing on a private investigation LaTurner had spearheaded in the murder case. LaTurner was a private investigator in 1977 and had no official part in the state investigation. Allegedly confiscated, according to the petition, was a plastic baggie containing a yellow latex glove with stains, an audio tape of a witness under hypnosis, three polygraph charts, witness's agreed to the polygraph exam; test questions of the witness and the letter stating the results of the exam. LaTurner said the OSBI wouldn't return anything, even though they felt the items had no significance to the case.[86]

May 31st, 1993 – Ella Mae Buckskin, Dies at age 67. Ella Mae was the mother of Gene Leroy Hart, she stood by her son and never wavered in support of him. She believed her son, "Sonny", was innocent in the deaths of the Girl Scouts.[87]

October 1st, 1994 – "Someone Cry for the Children" Documentary aired, for the first time, on cable television's Discovery Channel. The Tulsa filmmaker, Michael Wilkerson had been the lead agent for the Oklahoma State Bureau of Investigation at the time of the deaths at a Girl Scout camp near Locust Grove.[88]

June 8th, 1996 - Ted LaTurner former private investigator, said he had three suspects, an eyewitness and other evidence he believed prosecutors had missed. LaTurner tried to get authorities to reopen the case, and filed a petition seeking a grand jury to look into the murder investigation. He insisted the FBI should conduct DNA tests on two of the men. One assailant in the petition died in a Kansas prison, another had been released from Oklahoma's prison system after serving a sentence for second-degree murder; and the third man lived in eastern Oklahoma.[89]

June 11th, 1996 – Mayes County District Judge James Goodpaster invalidated Ted LaTurner's petition which called for a grand jury probe of investigators in the Girl Scout murder case. Goodpaster said the petition did not meet legal requirements. The petition alleged prosecutorial failure to interview unnamed eyewitness, review unspecified scientific evidence, and investigate and prosecute unspecified crimes committed by unnamed law enforcement officials.[90]

June 13th, 1996 – Ted LaTurner did not give up and re-filed his petition.[91]

June 15th, 1996 – Mayes County district judge certified the grand jury petition filed by Ted LaTurner, because it was legally sufficient to circulate. LaTurner had 45 days to gather approximately 340 signatures of registered voters in the county. However, Ted LaTurner faced jail time if he didn't pay the $775.40 balance he owed on a $1000 fine for a 1991 misdemeanor of operating as a private investigator without a license. LaTurner did pay fines.[92]

July 4th, 1996 – Ted LaTurner postponed efforts to initiate grand jury investigation, due to the fact that the law restricted impaneling a grand jury during general and primary elections. LaTurner didn't want to take chances that the grand jury would be dismissed before the investigation was completed. LaTurner had conducted a 15-year private investigation into the murders and had developed evidence leading to three suspects other than Gene Hart.[93]

November 16th, 1996 – Ted LaTurner refiled grand jury petition in the Mayes County court clerk's office. In the November 5th elections, voters had approved an increase in the number of signatures required, so LaTurner had to collect 500 signatures in 45 days. The signatures would then be turned over to the Election Board, which had 7 days to verify signatures; the judge would then have 30 days to empanel a jury. [94]

November 20th, 1996 – District judge approved Ted LaTurner's third attempt to get a grand jury petition. The Judge, Goodpaster, had to review State Question 670, which was approved by voters on the November 5th election, to determine how many registered voter signatures LaTurner had to obtain.[95]

December 25th, 1996 – A new law passed made Ted LaTurner need 1,934 signatures by January 2nd to impanel a grand jury. Before the law was passed he only needed 334 signatures from registered voters in the county. LaTurner supposedly already had over 2000 signatures.[96]

January 22nd, 1997 – Ted LaTurner missed deadline to submit his grand jury petition. The Judge had no plans to request a grand jury probe himself.[97]

February 24th, 1997 – Walter Milner, Doris Milner's father died on Valentine's Day at age 53. Retired 30+ year veteran of the Tulsa Police and Medal of Valor recipient, Milner died of a heart attack at his home and was buried beside his daughter Doris Milner.[98]

May 19th, 2002 – A reported 2001 DNA Testing failed to link Gene Leroy Hart to the crimes. Officials used a semen stained pillowcase from the crime scene; the semen was suspected to have been Hart's. FBI tested the same pillowcase in 1989 and the tests were inconclusive. Polymerase chain reaction/short tandem repeat test used to extract DNA from the pillowcase were not successful. The samples tested were insufficient and too deteriorated, but the investigators did retrieve a partial DNA profile of a female. However, the information was partial and not sufficient for comparison to the girls.[99]

July 8th, 2002 – "The Paper" an Oklahoma Newspaper reports that Ted LaTurner's petition named three possible suspects in the Girl Scout murders. In a grand jury petition, La Turner had named suspects Sonny James, Bill Stevens and Frank Justice, while an eyewitness, Minister Rev. Gerald Manley, reportedly saw James, Justice and two men he believed to be Stevens and Hart inside one of the tents on the night of the murders.[101]

It was also revealed in "The Paper" that Ted LaTurner had become overwhelmed and copped out, left town and started drinking. LaTurner left town in November 1996 before a grand jury could be called to investigate the murders. LaTurner, a former special deputy for Paul Smith assigned to investigate the murders in early 1980's, mysteriously disappeared without a trace in the fall of 1996. LaTurner returned to Oklahoma, cleaned up and had no plans to pursue support for another grand jury petition to reopen the Girl Scout murders. He didn't feel he had any hope of proving anyone wrong.[100]

July 8th, 2002 – Also reported by "The Paper", evidence was still being held at the old Mayes County Jail in Locust Grove, Oklahoma, which was serving as the county evidence locker in

2002. Three brown deteriorated grocery bags stacked on an old bunk were stapled shut and marked. The items inventory written on the outside of the bags included "dried blood samples from the victims".[102]

October 2003 – OETA, Oklahoma's statewide public media source, ran a documentary "Missing Pieces, Oklahoma Girl Scout Murders; June 13, 1977". A crime that remains unsolved haunts families, investigators and in Oklahoma case Prosecutors who tried to convict and lost.[103]

May 25th, 2007 - More testing began on DNA recovered from one of the victims with a known semen sample.[104]

June 25th, 2008 - DNA testing inconclusive, The Y-STR DNA analysis on the sperm fraction of the evidence, and DNA analysis of the epithelium (female) fraction of the evidence were conducted. No results obtained from the sperm fraction, but degraded partial DNA profile genetically typed as female was obtained from one of the pillowcase stains. Female DNA found could not be ruled out as coming from the victims. Tests to establish the DNA profile of the sexual assault were too deteriorated to obtain a DNA profile.[105]

February 25th, 2010 - Helen "Smitty" Gray dies at age 90. She was the former camp director at Camp Scott from 1970 until 1976. She was also called as a witness at the 1985 civil trial and had denied any warnings at Camp Scott before the murders.[106]

Girl Scout Murders Still Touching Lives

June 2011 - Book "Tent Number Eight" by attorney Gloyd McCoy, of Noble, was published, revisiting the tragic murders that happened in 1977 and the trial of Gene Hart, which followed.[107]

July 8th, 2011 - John Russell Penn, ex-con who admitted having "a checkered past," claimed he would reveal the true perpetrator of the infamous 1977 Girl Scout murders in his film.

Penn, named Karl Myers, who had admitted to the murders in a drunken stupor one night in 1978 while Penn and Russell were in the Ottawa County, Oklahoma, prison.[108]

July 12th, 2011 – Planned movie to solve the murders of three Girl Scouts expanded interest to the national media. The Oklahoma State Bureau of Investigations received phone calls asking if the OSBI was still on the case. An OSBI spokesman said that they continued to investigate the 1977 Girl Scout murder case due to the acquittal of the main suspect. Agents would continue to aggressively investigate leads that would provide answers for the victims' families. [109]

January 10th, 2012 – T. Jack Graves dies at age 85. As Rogers County's district attorney he was involved in Oklahoma's Girl Scout murder case and several other high-profile prosecutions. Graves assisted then-Tulsa County District Attorney Buddy Fallis in the prosecution of Gene Leroy Hart. He remained convinced throughout his life that Gene Hart was guilty.[110]

December 28th, 2012 – Karl Myers dies at age 64 at the Oklahoma State Penitentiary in McAlester, Oklahoma. According to the penitentiary, they found him unresponsive, while he was staying in the medical unit. He was sentenced to death in the murder of a Broken Arrow woman in 1996 and had been on death row since 1998. He served time in Oklahoma and Kansas for assault and rape before his conviction; he had also been connected to a rape and murder of another woman in 1993.

John Russell believed Myers was the man who molested and murdered the three girl scouts at Camp Scott in 1977.[111]

March 8th, 2014 – The Oklahoma State Bureau of Investigation reported they had continued work on the decades-old Girl Scout Murders case. Few criminal cases in Oklahoma had been as notorious as the Girl Scouts murdered in Locust Grove. Sometime in 2011 the OSBI Cold Case Unit, funded through a federal granted, reviewed the case and identified evidence that possibly would benefit from new forensic testing. The new Director authorized the comprehensive review of the entire case to identify any leads that could draw a clear conclusion to the case. The OSBI criminalists had tested more than 200 items of evidence using the most up-to-date forensic techniques available to the Bureau.

The National Center of Missing and Exploited Children agreed to help with the case. In 2013 the Mayes County Sheriff Mike Reed, the OSBI case agent, and the OSBI lab director traveled to Virginia to consult with NCMEC experts who reviewed the case and leads. A few pieces of evidence were submitted to a private lab for tests not currently available to the OSBI lab.

If the lab tests result in conclusive evidence of a suspect or suspects it might bring final justice for the families.[162]

3

THREE FAMILIES, THEIR LIVES CHANGED FOREVER

Murder of Girls at Scout Camp

The Guse Family

The Daily Times, Sunday, June 26th, 1977 - By Ron Grimsley reported.

On Monday June 13th at 11:45am, Richard Guse, father of Michele, received a call at work from his wife GeorgeAnn. With a quivering voice she told him Michele was dead. Richard immediately headed home to his wife, only knowing that his daughter was dead with no other details. Together they waited several long hours and finally heard the news about how their daughter had been murdered.

On Sunday, June 12th, at 2pm, they had put their only daughter on chartered bus to camp Scott. Michele was turning 10 on July 22 and the family had decided to buy Michele a 10-speed bicycle for her birthday, a gift she would never receive.

The first thing the Guse's did was call their family to tell them the terrible news of what had happened to Michele. Soon they would meet with their minister and go through the steps of selecting a funeral home, making arrangements and establishing a memorial fund instead of flowers.

Afraid they would never see their only daughter again, Richard and his wife decided they wanted to see Michele's body. On Wednesday morning, June 15th, the medical examiner released her body to the funeral home where Mr. and Mrs. Guse would finally able to see their daughter, for the last time that Wednesday night. They had ten wonderful years with Michele; she wanted to be a math teacher like her mother. Richard, GeorgeAnn and their son Mike 13, Michele's brother, said their final farewells at her Memorial service held at the Marlin Funeral home of Broken Arrow, Oklahoma on June 17th, 1977.

In the Guse's attic, Michele's sleeping bag and other possessions from the camp were stored. Michele's room remains much the same, including her prized African violets.

The family, while dealing with the stages of grief, became members of the Oklahoma Crime Victims Compensation Board and organized a local chapter of Compassionate Friends, a support group for parents who lost children. They felt working with the victims' groups would help them keep from feeling completely crazy.[112]

Michele Heather Guse, 9, was an excellent student, well-liked by others and an avid reader. She was shy, but had loved playing on a soccer team during fourth grade. She was a member of the local Girl Scouts J.J. Troop # 624 in Broken Arrow.

On the first night of camp, Michele wrote a letter to her Aunt Karen asking how she was and told how she was writing the letter from her tent at camp and how her tent was the very last tent in the unit. She finished by telling her aunt that the color of her bedroom was purple.[113]

Of the three murdered girls, Michele was the last to be laid to rest; her memorial service was held at Marlin Funeral home of Broken

Arrow, on Friday June 17th, 1977. It's believed her body was cremated soon after the service, and her ashes given to her family.

Michelle was born July 22nd, 1967; she died June 13th, 1977.

Girl Scouts bludgeoned

The Farmer Family

Friends of Dr. Charles and Sheri Farmer were listed as emergency contacts and the first to learn of Lori's death. The Magic Empire Council officials, unable to reach the Farmers, contacted them. The friends located the Farmer family and gave them the news of their daughter's death at Camp Scott.

Their friends also called Bonnie Brewster, Executive Director of the Magic Empire Council, and asked what had happened. Brewster would only say there was an accident. She said she was unable to say much more because she had been advised not to, but indicated there had been foul play.

Dr. Charles and Sheri Farmer had also tried to find out more about Lori's death, but the Magic Empire officials told the family that Bonnie Brewster would come visit them at their home soon to talk to them face to face. The family waited all day long, when Brewster and a Magic Empire Council attorney finally arrived; Brewster would not tell any of the circumstances surrounding

Lori's murder. Sheri even asked what her daughter had had for dinner at Camp Scott the night before, but Brewster said nothing about what she knew, and then left.

Sheri Farmer would learn more from the news media than she could from the Magic Empire council or the police investigating her daughter's death.[114]

Sheri would forever have to live with the fact that since her daughter Lori couldn't decide whether to attend the Girl Scout camp or a camp sponsored by the Tulsa area YMCA, Sheri would be the one to decide to send her daughter, the oldest of five children, to camp Scott the week of July 13th.

The first night at camp, Lori wrote a letter home that was never sent. The letter later found by investigators inside the tent, was addressed to her Mom, Dad, her sisters and her brother. She told them she was getting ready for bed and how she was having fun and had met two new friends, Michele Guse and Denise Milner and was sharing a tent with them. How it had started raining on the way back from dinner, and how she couldn't wait to write.[115]

Lori's mom sometimes wears Lori's heart shaped gold ring, on her own little finger to keep her close. Sheri is quick to correct anyone who says she has only four children, because they have five. They don't leave out Lori. Together as a family, they had learned to cope with Lori's brutal death. [116]

The Farmer family still feels the Girl Scout council should have been held accountable for the girls' safety and what happened to them.

Lori Lee Farmer, 8, was well liked and had a sweet personality. Her father, Charles Farmer, described Lori as an exceptional and bright child who, at 16 months old, suddenly recited the Pledge of Allegiance, flawlessly. Then, two months later, when she was 18 months old, recited the entire "Twas the Night Before Christmas." By the time Lori was 2 years old, she could work a 100-piece jigsaw puzzle, Lori would later, skip the second grade, after testing showed she had an IQ of 130 and a mental age of 10.[117]

Lori's 9th birthday would have been Sunday, June 19th, 1977, just six days after her first day at camp. The Farmer family had planned to come to the camp the day of her birthday so they could all celebrate together.

She would be the first buried, on Wednesday, June 15th, 1977.
Lori's memorial service was held at Asbury Methodist Church.
She was buried at Memorial Park Cemetery in Tulsa, OK. Born
June 18th, 1968; she died June 13th, 1977.

It should be noted.. Bonnie Brewster, Director of the Magic
Empire Council, accepted the position of Director in 1974. On
June 13th, 1977, Mrs. Brewster received the phone call, early
Monday morning, that there had been a tragedy at Camp Scott.
Soon after, she and her husband headed to the camp to determine
what had happened. While in the Director's office at Camp Scott,
unbeknownst the Bonnie, her husband Ralph started suffering
signs of an impending stroke. The next Sunday he had major
surgery that was a success. She attended all three funerals for
Doris, Michelle and Lori.[118]

Barbara Brewster supported the idea of never reopening Camp
Scott after the tragedies.

The Milner Family

In a 1997 interview with Doris' mother, Bettye Milner, she said she hadn't been able to visit her daughter's grave since the funeral. She didn't like to think about what had happened to her daughter, but rather dwell on her memories of the way she was. When her daughter was killed, it was the most unimaginable horror a mother could ever deal with. Bettye said her grief was more of an intense fear, the shock of knowing her child she had given birth to, helped and loved her for 10 years had something so horrible happen to her. Items Denise had taken with her to camp were sealed in a box, in a closet in the home, and Bettye had no intentions of opening the box because it was part of her daughter. In Bettye's Bible is the never mailed letter Denise wrote at camp.

In the letter, Denise told her mom that she didn't like camp, and how it had been raining. She also told her mom that she didn't want to stay at the camp for two weeks.

Bettye, in 1987, said she no longer thinks daily about Denise, except around the June anniversary and Christmas. When she laughs and visits with people she knows in herself she will never be the same person she once was.[119]

Doris Denise Milner, 10, sold Girl Scout Cookies to friends, neighbors and relatives, and finally saved enough money for her trip to camp. Doris's principal said she was one of the nicest little girls you'd ever want to talk with, described by teachers as a model student who received straight A's in the fourth grade and had been honored for having the highest achievement and best study habits in her class.[120]

Bettye described her daughter as an extremely friendly little girl, who loved people and "anywhere we went, she always made friends".

Denise taught herself to read and write at age 4, and any time she had a question about anything, she went to the library to look it up. She was especially interested in tap-dancing, skating and gymnastics, and studied each of those skills. She was a child that wanted to do so much and just tried to do everything she could do. Bettye said Denise dearly loved her younger sister, who was 5 at the time of Denise's death.[121]

June 16th, 1977 – In Tulsa Oklahoma, more than 300 mourners filed into the sanctuary of the Antioch Baptist Church, many friends and family said their goodbyes with questions not answered about what had happened. Doris was the second to be buried of the three killed; she was buried at Green Acres Memorial Gardens in Sperry, OK.[122]

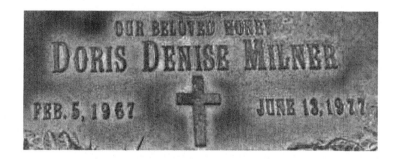

In 1997 **Walter Milner**, Doris's father, who was a retired Tulsa Police veteran of 31 years and a medal of valor recipient, died of a heart attack on February 24th, at the age of 53.

Milner was hired by the Tulsa Police Department on March 16, 1965.

During his years of service, Milner worked as a patrolman for the city's uniform division.

On June 10, 1996, Milner was one of several officers who engaged in a downtown gunfight in which a robbery suspect and a fellow officer were killed, and another officer was injured.

The Oklahoma Association of Chiefs of Police presented Milner with a medal of valor during a ceremony on August 1996 and on Oct 31st he retired from his work in the Tulsa Uniform Division North.

Milner, who was preceded in death by his 10-year-old daughter, Doris was buried next to her.[123]

4

CAMP SCOTT

The 410 acre camp was named in honor of H.J. "Scotty" and Florence Scott, who were both Tulsa Boy and Girl Scout volunteers. They donated 24 acres in 1928 for the core of the camp to open. The Oklahoma Girl Scout Council, through the years, would use money raised by selling Girl Scout cookies to buy additional land.

In the spring of 1956 Girl Scouts planted thousands of pine trees throughout the camp. In 1962, the Tulsa Civitan Club underwrote the construction of Camp Scott's Great Hall facility and the materials needed for the building would come from cookie sales. Money was also donated by the civic clubs throughout Oklahoma to build several other smaller buildings on the land. From 1928 till June 13th, 1977, over 12,000 girls attended camp Scott.[124]

Camp Scott was arranged into twelve campsites, each unit named after Indian Tribes: Osage, Chickasaw, Creek, Seminole, Choctaw, Comanche, Cherokee, Arapahoe, Quapaw and Kiowa.

There were eight wooden platform tents at each of the Kiowa, Arapahoe, Quapaw, Choctaw, Quapaw units and four wooden platform tents at both the Seminole, Comanche units, while wooden cabins were at the Osage, Chickasaw, and Creek units. The two winterized cabins where the Cedar Lodge and the Red Barn.

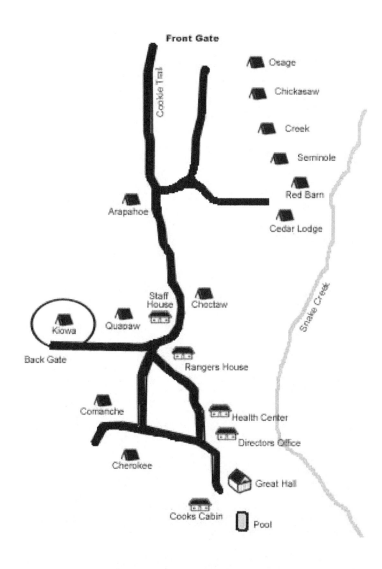

Map of Camp Scott in 1977

Wooden platform tents used at Camp Scott

Kiowa Campsite Layout

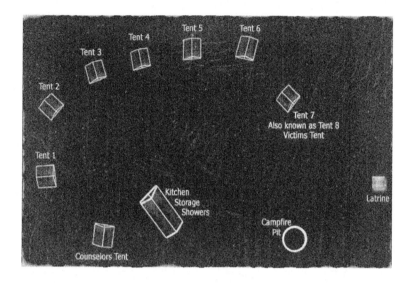

December 6th, 1977 – The Magic Empire Girl Scout Council announced Camp Scott would not be reopened until redesigned to make it safer. The changes would include new security measures with added camp security personnel, clearing away dense wooded areas and relocation of the campsite units. The target reopen date was for the 1979 camping season.[125]

On June 13th, 1982 – The camp was still closed and reopening of Camp Scott, per Magic Empire Council was a 50/50 chance. By 1987 the camp had stayed closed and several acres on the south side of the camp were sold to a local farmer.[126]

Finally, on August 29th, 1988, It was announced that the Scout Board was selling the camp. 11 years after the unsolved Girl Scout murders, the Tulsa based council would not be using the site. The land had been on the market for several months and a for sale sign was put up on the property July 1988.[127]

Dan Scott, son of H.J. "Scotty" and Florence Scott, said the camp closing was another part of the tragedy and he would have liked to have seen the camp reopen.[128]

The land was finally bought by a new owner, JT Rowland who wanted to renovate the swimming pool and several of the buildings to reopen the area as a campground. After several attempts to keep the pool open to the public, the owner closed the campground, locked the gates and posted private property signs. Still owned by the same family, it is private property where people live, and the land is leased out to hunters during hunting season. JT Rowland passed away in 2014 and the land is now owned by his children.

5

INCIDENTS AT CAMP SCOTT
BEFORE JUNE 1977

The Camp Ranger, Ben Woodward, who was the caretaker and lived at Camp Scott, found a slashed tent flap with a four to five square inch section removed sometime during the hours before the scouts arrived Sunday.

On the Saturday before the camp session opened, the Camp Director's husband, Richard Day, came across a stranger walking around the camp carrying a clear plastic jug.[130]

One of the camp counselors reported two incidents during the week before camp began. Two staff members were followed one night by someone with a flashlight, and in yet another incident, a staff member saw a man enter their tent.[130]

Camp Scott counselor, Michelle Hoffman, found a threatening note in the camp's Seminole unit, less than two months before the murders.

On April 1ˢᵗ, 1977 a cabin where two Tulsa troop leaders were staying was ransacked, and $53 was taken. The Girl Scout leaders promptly cut the weekend encampment by one day. Also, in the summer of 1976 a peeping tom incident had been reported.[131]

Note: More incidents are covered in the section "Parents' lawsuit goes to trial".

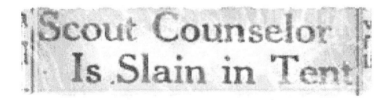

Camp Murder in Colorado 14 years before Camp Scott

Colorado Scout Margaret Elizabeth Beck, 16, from Denver, was slain 14 years before the murders at Camp Scott. In 1963, Margaret was found dead in her sleeping bag at the Mile-Hi Girl Scout camp.

The teenager slept alone in a tent the last night of a five-day outing for the scouts. Her tent companion had spent the night in the infirmary due to a cold.

Camp personnel noticed no signs of violence and initially thought the girl, whose body was in a zipped up sleeping bag, had choked in her sleep or had heart failure.

Before the sheriff arrived on the scene, camp leaders had cleaned everything up in her tent, packed her clothes and swept up in an attempt to keep from scaring the other campers.

When the sleeping bag was unzipped, officials discovered Margaret had been sexually assaulted and murdered.

Officials questioned over 300 people and believed one of them was the killer, but without physical evidence, no arrests were ever made.[129]

C.S. Kelly

6

TROUBLING EVENTS AFTER JUNE 1977

Girl Scout Drug From Tent In Sarasota, Fla.

On June 29th, 1977, a Girl Scout was dragged from a tent in Sarasota, Florida during a Campout.

During a campout at the Oscar Scherer State Park, a 15 year old Girl Scout was grabbed from her tent, by the hair of her head, and dragged into the thick underbrush of the state park. A heavy set man had ripped open the back of the tent and grabbed the girl before dawn. Two other girl scouts in the same tent screamed which awoke the leader of the Campout, who reported the abduction to the sheriff's office. Sheriff Deputies found a trail of boot prints and prints of bare feet leading to the old plant nursery. The camp leader and approximately 16 girls were all on a camping trip when this occurred on the first night.[133]

On June 30th, 1977 it's reported that the abducted 15 year old telephoned her father to say she was safe. Her father received the call 17 hours after the girl was dragged from the tent. The girl did not sound alarmed and told her father that she was all right and would be released soon.[134]

On July 3rd, 1977 the abducted Girl Scout, Charlotte Grosse, was released unharmed, and the man who abducted her was in custody. She was released 53 hours after being abducted from her tent.[135]

Tennis shoes appeared at Camp Scott

At the end of July 1977, a pair of tennis shoes appeared at Camp Scott, with the handwritten name of Denise Milner inside the shoes. The shoes were found on the front steps of the building formerly used as the command post by law enforcement after the murders, by the on-site security guards who were posted at Camp Scott after law enforcement had vacated the area. When the guards returned from searching the nearby woods where they had seen a silhouette of a man, they found the shoes which they had not seen until after returning. Tracking dogs were brought in but lost the trail, Investigators tied thread between trees near the murder scene which had been broken, and footprints had also been found. The shoes, which were found with a pair of socks inside a heavy plastic bag, were taken to the state crime lab for testing.[13]

In 2014 Denise Milner's mother refuted the newspaper claims and said the shoes were not Denise's.

7

GIRL SCOUT CAMPING AFTER CAMP SCOTT

The Tulsa-based, Magic Empire Council, didn't have a traditional summer camp from the time of the murders until four years later in 1981, when it acquired land on the Zink Ranch in Osage County for Camp Tallchief.

At the new camp, scouts stayed in raised cabins rather than in tents, with fewer trees surrounding the cabins. A large fence with barbed wire along the top surrounds the camp, with professional security on-site and plans in place for medical and law enforcement personnel to provide security and quick response. Prospective staff members are screened and attend mandatory training which include health, safety and emergency procedures.

Neither the parents nor visitors are allowed to show up unannounced during the camp sessions.

8

PARENTS' LAWSUIT GOES TO TRIAL

Murdered scouts' parents sue

Eight years after the state and country were shocked by the brutal slaying, on March 19, 1985, the trial of the civil lawsuit began at the Tulsa District Court.

Dr. Charles A. and Sherri Farmer and Walter and Bettye Milner said it was the negligence of the scout council and insurance company which allowed their daughters' deaths. Each family asked for $2.5 million in actual and punitive damages. In 1977, shortly after the murders, the families filed suit against the Magic Empire Council and its insurance agents, Hartford Insurance Company.

Attorneys for the families argued that the Magic Empire Council operated the camp without providing adequate security necessary to prevent the killings. The attorneys also implied that the Hartford Company opened itself up to liability when it inspected the camp before signing a liability policy with the Magic Empire Council. Six

men and six women were selected to be a jury to hear the case.

The trial began six years after a Mayes County jury found Gene

Leroy Hart not guilty of the murders.[136]

The Magic Empire Girl Scout Council's Camp Scott; was the camp

a well-run, wilderness retreat which tragically became the site of a

horrible, but unavoidable murder spree? Or was it an inadequately

staffed, unprotected, overgrown location in which strangers,

thieves and, ultimately, killers roamed at will?

The attorneys opened the first day of testimony in the lawsuit with

those two choices.

They argued that Camp Scott's staff remained relaxed about

security at the heavily wooded campground, despite intrusions and

theft over the years.

The number of incidents on the campground in the years before

the murders should have warned of the need for better security,

and Camp officials should have reported the incidents to local

authorities.

Once, a man was found inside campers' tents while, on another

occasion, someone tried to break into a cabin as the girls inside

screamed for help. Later a camper discovered a note warning that

three girls would be killed.

The attorney for the Magic Empire Council explained that many of

the intrusions were, in fact, sightings of local sportsmen or camp staff members. Most were obviously Girl Scout pranks, in the camp's 49 years of existence.

Camp officials believed contacting local authorities seemed unnecessary at the time in 1977.

Glenn "Pete" Weaver, who was Mayes County sheriff in 1977, said Gene Hart had been seen at his mother's house, just a mile from the camp. On other occasions, Hart had been sighted within miles of the camp.

On June 12th, 1977, the day the girls arrived at the camp, Weaver was investigating the second burglary of a farmhouse near the camp.

Weaver realized only after the killings that there was no security at Camp Scott. The Kiowa tents were in an unlighted, heavily wooded and overgrown location. The tent the girls were murdered in could not be seen from the camp counselors' tent allowing the killer or killers to assault and murder them without ever being detected.[137]

Several witnesses testified about countless intrusions, thefts, and burglaries at the camp over the years. Former counselors and campers had never been told what to do if intruders entered the camp.

Constance Cunningham, a former head counselor, testified that in a summer session in 1971, she borrowed a gun and stayed in a tent which had been entered the night before by a strange man, a situation that was the culmination of two years of frightening intrusions. During her two years as a counselor, tents were ransacked on several occasions, and intruders had been seen at night in the camp.

Cunningham had talked to camp director Helen "Smitty" Gray in 1970, about campers who had come to her about hearing heavy breathing outside their tents at night. Gray brushed it off because numerous things had gone on in past summers, and nothing had ever happened.

The next year, before summer sessions, Gray had a meeting with the counselors who knew about the incidents from the past years and cautioned them not to say anything to the new counselors, because she didn't want them to get upset. She wanted it to stay a secret.

Later that summer, a series of disturbing incidents began at the Kiowa unit. One counselor reported hearing a man's voice calling, "Help me. Help me. Please help me. I'm hurt." Later, someone ransacked tents, and counselors reported this to Gray.
"Gray again said, "It's nothing,"' Gray wasn't sure that some of the counselors weren't just playing a big joke.
As the intrusions continued, Cunningham grew more scared, but the camp directors pushed it aside and Gray insisted that it had

gone on in summers past, that no harm had been done, and not to worry about it.

In a March, 1981, deposition from a former Camp Scott counselor, Michelle Hoffman, testified about finding a threatening note in the camp's Seminole unit, less than two months before the murders. During a pre-summer prep session for volunteers, one of Hoffman's fellow counselors had found her belongings had been gone through; Hoffman said a box of doughnuts belonging to the counselor had been stolen. She later found the empty doughnut box and picked it up. She found a note inside, written on folded notebook paper.

In capital printed letters, "We are on a mission to kill three girls in tent one.' signed "The Killer"."

Hoffman said the note was alarming at first, but she decided it was a joke. She said the counselors turned the note over to Barbara Olmstead, coordinator of the spring Camporee session at Camp Scott. Olmstead threw the note away.

Olmstead testified that when the counselors gave her the note, they did not tell her that the tent had been ransacked.[138]

Girl Scout officials testified that, despite the recommendations of two groups that accredited Camp Scott, Tulsa's Magic Empire Girl Scout Council did not have a written security plan for the camp when the three young girls were raped and murdered. But camp officials had been well-versed in emergency procedures, even without written guidelines, testified Barbara Day, camp director at the time of the slayings.

Bonnie Brewster, Magic Empire executive director, testified that council officials planned for every sort of emergency they could imagine. She believed they were prepared for resident camp, but not prepared for murder. Camp officials planned security that would protect the girls from normal camp type things that happen in camp. Not in their wildest imagination would believe anything as heinous as murder could have ever happened at Camp Scott. Security provisions were in place, the camp's main gate was kept locked at night, and all campers were kept on a buddy system. Barbara Day testified that after taking over the camp, she notified the police in nearby Locust Grove that the summer camp was in session. Earlier witnesses testified that when they reported problems at the camp to Locust Grove police, the officers told them the camp was outside their jurisdiction.

Former Mayes County Sheriff Pete Weaver testified that the camp fell under the jurisdiction of the Mayes County Sheriff's Office. But Day said Locust Grove police advised her not to call the sheriff's office if the camp needed police help.

Barbara Day said she also introduced herself to Oklahoma Highway Patrol Trooper Harold Berry. She said Berry had "routinely" walked through the 410-acre camp to check on campers' safety in the past.

She told him the camp would welcome his continued surveillance. Paul J. Thompson, a Tulsa security expert, who was security director for American Airlines in Tulsa and former presidential bodyguard, testified that he felt several basic security improvements at Camp Scott would have deterred the killer. He felt camp's operators failed to take "common sense" security measures and security problems were particularly acute in the Kiowa unit, where the three tent mates were slain. The seven tents were spread so far apart that only two of them were clearly visible from the counselors' tent. Thompson also felt that the camp kitchen in the center of the unit obscured the view of campers' tents from the counselors' tent. The most obscured was the tent where the three murdered girls slept, the furthest from the counselors' tent and most remote unit in the camp.

Thompson testified that the camp should have maintained all-night watches in each unit. Each unit should have been surrounded by a wire, hung with bells, which would have signaled the approach of an intruder.

He felt the camp should also have had at least one armed security officer on patrol each night, with each counselor's tent equipped with a telephone or two-way radio, and the camp headquarters should have had a base station with which it could communicate with police and security officers.

Day said counselors did have walkie-talkies, but a camp base station was not working.

Thompson said tents should have been closely arranged in a circle, clearly visible to the counselor's tent. Thompson said each unit should have had a pole-mounted security light, and each tent should have been equipped with a light, along with a bell for summoning counselors.[139]

Barbara Day, who was the new director in 1977 at Camp Scott, said she could not have directed the camp if she had known it had a history of intrusions, burglaries and thefts in the years preceding the murders.

Neither Barbara Day nor former Camp Scott Counselor Dee Elder had known of any prior problems at the camp and had no reason to think any danger lurked in the woods.

Frances Hesselbein, executive director of the Girl Scouts, U.S.A. National Council, testified that since the murders, 200,000 girls had taken part in Girl Scout camping nationwide without tragedy recurring. In the 73-year history of Girl Scouting 30 million girls took part in the camping programs. In searching the records, there had been no incident in which a camper has been harmed by an intruder on the camp site.

Hesselbein admitted on cross-examination, however, that a camper was once kidnapped from a Florida camp.

The Girl Scout official testified, "the purposes of Girl Scout camps would be defeated by security measures, and the need to protect the environment and only make little changes to the natural environment as possible," she said.

The parents' attorneys argued that a number of incidents in the years preceding the murders should have warned Magic Empire officials of the need to improve camp security. The attorneys said camp operators should have cleared the timber and underbrush from the campsites, and should have installed fencing and outdoor security lights. Individual tents should also have been lighted; they argued.

Hesselbein said that a natural, outdoor setting is a central part of Girl Scout camping, and with ably trained counselors and staff they could maintain an essential outdoor program for girls. [140]

Helen "Smitty" Gray, former director of a Mayes County Girl Scout camp testified that she didn't remember the pattern of thefts, burglaries and intrusions in the years preceding the slayings even though several witnesses for the plaintiffs testified that they either told Gray of incidents or reported them in writing.

Constance Cunningham, a former head counselor at the camp, testified that in 1970, campers and counselors spied a man inside the camp and the camp's ranger-caretaker was not at home. A nearby resident came to the camp and walked through the woods firing his gun to frighten off intruders.

Gray did remember a neighbor bringing a .22-caliber rifle and firing two rounds into the woods after two counselors reported seeing an intruder. But she later found out the two girls had just made up the story for entertainment.

Gray said it was common for campers and counselors to get spooked, because normally children don't sleep outside, and that threatening notes and other pranks were very common at Camp Scott.

Gray said that the camp would occasionally be entered at night by area teens, or by the youths from a nearby Boy Scout camp, who were bent on pulling pranks inside the campground. But she disputed witnesses' claims that adult intruders had entered the camp.

Gray was asked if she remembered a woman named June Scoggins reporting a man entering a tent at night during a troop Campout. She said she was not responsible for all the individual troop camps and would not be the first one they came to talk to in Tulsa. June Scoggins testified that she repeatedly told Gray and other Magic Empire officials of an August 1975 incident at Camp Scott. Scoggins said that weeks later she inquired about the incident during a training session, and they told her they were not going to do anything about it because they didn't want to cause panic. Marge Scanlin, Director of Standards and Field Services for the American Camping Association testified that the ACA had not changed campground-accreditation standards as a result of the 1977 murders because there were no standards that could be written that would prevent an unforeseeable criminal action.[141]

On March 27th, 1985, Jurors deliberated nearly five hours before arriving at a verdict. They found that the murders of three Girl

82

Scouts at Camp Scott near Locust Grove in June 1977, were not the result of negligence on the part of the Magic Empire Girl Scout Council or its insurance company. After five hours of deliberation, the jury ruled by a 9-3 vote, in favor of the Magic Empire Council and the Hartford Accident and Indemnity Company.[142]

May 7th, 1985, A request for a new trial was rejected when attorneys for the families had sought a new trial after jurors found the Magic Empire Council was not liable. The attorneys felt the Council's attorneys had gone beyond the scope of the issues and evidence during the trial. The attorneys had 30 days to appeal Tulsa County Special District Judge William R. Beasley.

In June 1985, the parents decided to file for an appeal to the Oklahoma Supreme Court ruling.[143]

In December 1986, the State Court of Appeals upheld the 1985 decision that the Magic Empire Council of Girl Scouts and its insurance company were not liable for the murders.[161]

9

DNA TESTING OVER THE YEARS

On July 26th, 1989, The FBI lab used cutting-age genetic testing in which evidence underwent a procedure called "DNA fingerprinting". The technique was developed in 1987 and the FBI began using it in December 1988.

The new test analyzed blood and/or semen, based on the fact that no two people share exactly the same genetic makeup. At the time, scientists indicated there was 85 to 90 percent chance that the test results would be inconclusive, but the FBI made a special exception in the case of the Girl Scout killings, breaking a rule that it accepts only active cases.

DNA fingerprinting was a highly sophisticated method in the late 80's; a method of identifying people using these DNA tests would genetically link stained evidence with suspect's identification. These techniques, which took eight weeks, allowed the isolation of DNA from body fluids such as blood, semen and saliva, chemically extracted from stained materials. Evidence used by the FBI included a pillowcase stained with seminal fluid, as well as a known blood sample from Gene Hart.[144]

On August 2nd, 1989, Oklahoma State officials acted against the recommendation of the deputy assistant director of the FBI's Laboratory Division, because the FBI lab had not matched DNA on evidence older than five years and the samples were more than 12 years old. They suggested sending evidence to Cetus Laboratories of Emeryville, California. Cetus had developed a DNA test designed for the analysis of old or degraded DNA. The test would not identify a killer, but would either exclude or prove if Gene Leroy Hart was the attacker.[145]

On October 25th, 1989, the deoxyribonucleic acid DNA tests of Gene Hart's body fluids were too inconclusive.

The tests conducted showed one in 7,700 American Indians would match the sample of body fluids taken from the crime scene, but the results were inconclusive.[146]

In 2002, more DNA tests were conducted to extract DNA from the same pillowcase used for DNA tested in 1989 and again were not successful. The samples tested were insufficient and too deteriorated.

The polymerase chain reaction/short tandem repeat DNA test was used, which had a good track record with old, deteriorated evidence. But even after trying twice to get the genetic markers, both tests were unsuccessful.

Investigators did retrieve a partial DNA profile of a female, but the information was partial and not sufficient for comparison to rule out the murdered girls.[147]

In 2007, an independent laboratory used by the Oklahoma State Bureau of Investigation compared DNA recovered from one of the victims with a known semen sample from Gene Leroy Hart. The lab used up an entire piece of evidence which was destroyed by the proceedings. The Y-STR DNA analysis on the sperm fraction of the evidence, and DNA analysis of the epithelium (female) fraction of the evidence were conducted. No results were obtained from the sperm fraction, but degraded partial DNA profile genetically typed as female was obtained from one of the pillowcase stains. Female DNA found could not be ruled out as coming from the victims. Tests to establish a DNA profile from the sexual assault samples were too deteriorated to obtain a DNA profile.[148]

10

ANNIVERSARY OF THE MURDERS

March 30th, 1980 - The Cedar Rapids Gazette reported:

"Girl Scout slayings still a mystery"

A year had passed since the jurors stunned the nation by announcing Gene Hart was innocent of the first degree murders. But the verdict left the unanswered question: Who was guilty? The 410 acre camp had remained locked since confused Girl Scouts were evaluated the first day of a two week encampment. The triple murder remained an open case in the Oklahoma State Bureau of Investigation files, officially unsolved, but the investigation had come to a standstill since the trial.[149]

June 13th, 1982 - The Daily Oklahoman reported:

"Girl Scout Slayings 5 Years Ago Still Haunt Families"

When the sun came up, camp counselor came across a scene that stunned the nation. The Girl Scouts dragged from their tent and killed. Memories had faded for some, but not for the families of the girls, because their experience was still very real.

Walter Milner tried not to dwell on the murders every day, but birthdays and holidays were difficult.

The families wondered if the killer was alive or dead, since Gene Hart, who was arrested for the murders, had had a month long trial, was found innocent, and died two months later of a heart attack at age 35.

Milner didn't know if Hart was the killer, but it would be easier to think Hart was guilty. He just didn't know.[150]

June 26th, 1988 - The Daily Oklahoman Reported:
"Families Cope with Death of Children"

Charles and Sheri Farmer had lived with "Shock, anger and bitterness" for 11 years since daughter was killed. June brought back horrible memories. Sheri Farmer couldn't forget Lori's senseless death; it affected the whole family who missed her daily. To make things worse, the counselors in charge of the Farmers' daughter at Camp Scott had never spoken to them.

Even after eleven years Richard Guse, father of Michelle, felt life would never be the same because the pain was the same as the day she was killed.

The calendar in Michelle's room reads June 1977. Her toys and books were packed away, but her room basically remained the same. Not a shrine, but no reason to change or redecorate it.

Michelle's older brother, now 24, had refused to discuss his sister's death with his parents since it happened.[151]

June 9th, 1997 - Tulsa World Reported:

"Murders put Council, Families in Different worlds"

The murders triggered the sale of Camp Scott and upgraded security measures at the new camp.

Magic Empire Council of the Girl Scouts had not had a traditional camp for four years after the murders. The new camp had better security with security guards and fences around the camp with barbed wire along the top.[152]

June 9th, 1997 - Tulsa World Reported:

"20 Years Later, Slayings at Camp Still Shock, Horrify"

20 years ago at Camp Scott, on a stormy night, a tent with three girls asleep were raped and murdered, and the killer vanished into the darkness. Innocence was lost, and everyone was stunned by the violence with no conclusion, the horror of finding the bodies, the manhunt for Gene Leroy Hart, the prosecution, the defense and finally the verdict of, not guilty.[153]

June 9th, 1997 – Tulsa World Reported:

"Elusive Truth // Speculation Still Rampant 20 Years After Slayings"

Friday marked the 20th anniversary of the murders; speculation still ran rampant and the truth still elusive. Sheri Farmer, Lori's mother, thought they would find out what happened, but not sure anymore. In 1997, the Farmers ended the Parents of Murdered Children chapter they founded in Tulsa and deciding it was time to move on, but would never stop searching for the truth about Lori's death. Bettye Milner, Denise's mother, had not visited her daughter's grave since the funeral, because she could not bring herself to go. Michelle Guse's family gave no response to requests for an interview.[154]

June 9th, 2002 - the Tulsa World reported:

"Shadow of a doubt"

After 25 years, the case still controversial and the three girls' names still linked to one of the worst crimes in eastern Oklahoma history. Sheri Farmer, Lori's mother thought back to how she had worried about the bus ride to the camp and felt relieved when she had checked the clock and realized the bus would be at the camp. The Farmers were still searching for answers.[155]

June 13th, 2002 - The Daily Oklahoman Reports:

"Girl Scout Killings Still Haunt State"

What happened twenty-five years ago haunted Oklahoma and parents no longer felt children were safe. The three girls' murders left behind questions that could not be answered.

Sheri Farmer, Lori's mother, wished someone would come forward and tell her who killed her daughter, because Lori's death remained open ended for her.[156]

June 13th, 2007, Tulsa World Reports:

"Mom keeps low profile on girl's murder anniversary"

The 30th anniversary, Bettye Milner, mother of Doris, tried to treat the day as any other day. Attorney Garvis Isaacs, who represented Hart in the 1979 Girl Scout Murder trial, still believed Hart was innocent, but S.M. "Buddy" Fallis, who prosecuted the case, was still convinced of Hart's guilt.

Bettye Milner kept a low profile because nothing had changed, nothing new had been learned and there were no new suspects.[157]

June 17th, 2007, The Oklahoman Reports:

"1977 killings changed the face of security at summer camps"

Summer Camp changed 30 years ago after the three Girl Scouts were murdered at Camp Scott. It caused nightmares and people locked their doors because of the loss of innocence[158]

June 26th, 2008, Tulsa World Reports:

"No DNA clues – Link not found in Scout murders"

Science had made a lot of progress in 30 years, but not enough to help solve the murders. DNA testing found no conclusive evidence. The three families and the public had no new answers, after 30 years, about the murders because scientific tests had limits.[159]

June 29th, 2008, The Oklahoman Reports:

"Murder case's lore, mystery keeps growing"

After thirty-one years, debate still over continued if Hart murdered the three Girl Scouts. Hart remained the only person charged, and he had been acquitted. When Hart died the truth might have died with him. He died of a heart attack in 1979 at the Oklahoma State Penitentiary in McAlester while serving time for rape, burglary and kidnapping charges, not related to the Girl Scout case.

Theories of other suspects and opinions about the case could still be found on internet forums and websites.[160]

11

THE 1978 PRELIMINARY HEARING OF
THE FIRST DEGREE MURDER CHARGES

On the 7th of June, 1978 at approximately 10:00 AM, a preliminary
hearing began for the Criminal Felony Proceedings of the First
Degree murder charges against Gene Leroy Hart in the case of the
Girl Scout Murders at Camp Scott. These are the notes taken
directly from the original transcript detailing the viewpoint of the
Camp Counselors, Director, and campers and what they had seen
and heard. Additionally, this document includes the evidence that
had been seen and collected by the authorities who were called to
the crime scene on June 13th, 1977, and the days that followed.

These notes are not about Gene Hart, but rather the evidence and
firsthand accounts from those who were present at Camp Scott.

Dee Ann Elder, 1st witness called to the stand on June 7th, 1978
Dee Ann Elder served as the Unit Leader of the Kiowa Unit
campsite, and she was one of three counselors in charge of the
unit.

On Monday June 2nd, the week before camp started, Dee Elder attended the 5 day pre-camp, staff-only training at Camp Scott. On Friday afternoon of that week, she personally checked all the tents in the Kiowa unit, and made a list of tent repairs needed before camp started that coming Sunday afternoon. She then left the camp, and returned to Tulsa, Oklahoma on that Friday night, June 6th.

On Sunday, June 12th Dee returned to Camp Scott in the mid-afternoon. Upon visiting the Kiowa unit, she noticed that a tent flap on one of the tents appeared damaged, and possibly even slashed. She reported the damage to get it repaired.

Prior to the arrival of children, Barbara Day, the Camp Director, gave Dee and the other Unit Leaders a roster with a list of the children who had been assigned to each unit during the next two weeks. At around 3:00 PM, Greyhound buses began delivering campers, and children were sorted and directed to the various units according to age.

At approximately 4:00 PM, the Kiowa Unit children, seven to ten years of age, were taken to their campsite area and they met in the unit kitchen. The children were then shown the seven tents, each containing our cots. Campers were allowed to choose a tent and with whom they wanted to bunk. The campers then reported back to Dee Elder their choices, and a chart was made outlining who was in each tent.

At around 5:30PM, thirty minutes before supper, six girls were chosen from each camp unit and taken to the Great Hall. Here, they were assigned as "hoppers" and they set up the tables for dinner. At around fifteen minutes to six, all the remaining children were then taken to the Great Hall for supper.

After supper, the campers and camp staff moved to the Great Hall's front porch, and Dee Elder led the group in camp songs until it had started storming and raining heavily. At this time, the campers were dismissed and they returned to their respective campsites.

Once back at the Kiowa Unit, Dee instructed the campers to go to their tents to change into dry clothes. She then went to each tent in order to hock the flaps down for rainy weather. This was accomplished by around 7:00 PM.

Dee Elder returned to the Great Hall to retrieve cookies while the campers were still in their tents. When she returned to the Kiowa Unit, she gathered the children under the unit kitchen shelter to review camp rules, and the children were assigned camp duties for that coming week. They sang camp songs and ate the cookies. Dee then instructed the children to go to their various tents and get ready for bed. At around 10:00PM, Dee Elder visited each tent and talked to the children to ensure they were okay, warm, and had enough blankets.

Before and during 1977, Camp Scott had no lights in the wooden platform tents. Aside from the campers' flashlights, the only light source provided at the camp units were the kerosene lanterns which were lit at night. These lanterns hung at the unit latrines.

On that first night of the camp session, Dee was the counselor assigned to remain at the unit, called "sitting hill", while the other 2 counselors, Carla Wilhite and Susan Emery left the unit for a two hour break. Around 11:00PM, Carla and Susan returned and settled in for the night in the Counselors' tent which all three counselors' shared. The children, on the other hand, remained noisy most of the time. At around 1:30AM, both Dee and Susan heard the unit's latrine door slam. Carla left the counselor's tent in order to escort the noisy girls back to their tent.

At approximately 6:00AMam, Monday morning, June 13th, 1977, Carla's alarm wakened Dee, but she decided to stay in bed and sleep a while longer. After Carla left the tent to take a hot shower at the staff house, Dee fell back to sleep only to be awakened by Carla returning and yelling that they "need to count the kids." Carla did not say why, but Dee jumped up and followed Carla out of the counselors' tent asking her what was going on. Carla told her there was something in the road, and they needed to check on the children at which time Dee ran to tent number 7 while Carla and Susan headed to tent number1 to check on the children. They would then meet in the middle at tent #3 or #4.

Upon Dee's arrival at tent #7, all three children were gone. Dee called out to the other two counselors, reporting that the kids were missing. Carla and Susan ran to tent #7, and stood there for a moment trying to determine where the children might be. They then noticed there were no sleeping bags or mattress covers on the three cots and also saw blood on the floor. Initially, Dee did not think anything bad had happened, but perhaps a nosebleed was the cause of the blood, and perhaps the children were in another tent.

The counselors then regrouped and counted the children in the remaining tents, but three little girls were still unaccounted for. Suddenly, Susan Emery screamed. She had just walked over and saw a dead child lying on the ground. Dee ran up to Susan and told her to be quiet so as not to wake the other children. Dee told Susan to stay in the unit while she went for help.

Dee went to her car which was parked at the Staff House and went to the Camp Director's Office to find Barbara Day. On the way, she met Mary Ann Alaback, the camp nurse, who was heading toward the Kiowa Unit in her own car. She stopped to ask Dee what was wrong, and Dee replied that something horrible had happened, that she thought some of the children were dead and that Mary should get down to the Unit. Dee then continued to the Camp Director's office, where Barbara, her husband Richard, and Carla were already in the camps' station wagon and headed to the Kiowa area. Dee returned her car to the Staff House and walked back to the Kiowa Unit where the station wagon was parked near the body. She stood by the car as Barbara Day came over and confirmed what Dee already knew: three children were dead. Dee then realized she needed to get the sleeping children up and out of the Kiowa Unit tents and away from the area. Before doing this, she went to the Quapaw Unit to waken her close friend Linda Henderson and inform her of the terrible news. She then had helped Linda count the kids in the Quapaw Unit. Dee rushed back to the Kiowa area and devised a plan to get the children up and out of the area by a back road.

The sleepy children did as they were told, and none of the children had any idea what had happened. They were kept busy until being taken to the Great Hall for an early breakfast with the rest of the camp. During breakfast, all three Kiowa Unit counselors were called to the Director's office and questioned by the State Police. After breakfast, the Kiowa Unit children were taken to the craft hut where they were occupied with various activities. Later on, the children were questioned as to whether they had seen or heard anything the previous night, but none had.

Dee continued to answer questions from the authorities. After the children were placed on buses around 3:00PM to go back to Tulsa, Oklahoma, all of Camp Scott's staff met in the Great Hall Bonnie Brewster, President of the Girl Scout Council, would be the first to speak to the group. She told them the camping sessions were suspended, and the staff would need to leave that evening. After, one of the Officers in charge spoke to them. At around 4:30PM a law enforcement officer spoke with Dee again, and at 5:00PM Dee was allowed to leave camp for the evening. Dee returned to Camp Scott on Tuesday June 14th, where she was interviewed at the Great Hall by the OSBI. Dee and the other two Kiowa counselors were taken by Law enforcement officers to the Counselor's tent in the Kiowa Unit. There, they were asked to inventory their personal property before gathering their items to take home with them. Dee found nothing missing, and was allowed to take her belongings and leave the camp. The next day, June 15th, she was asked again to return, and answered more questions. She also provided a hair sample, a saliva sample, fingerprints and had her picture taken. Dee continued to be interviewed on several more occasions throughout and after June 1977.[164]

Carla Wilhite, 2nd witness called to the stand on June 7th, 1978.
Carla Wilhite, one of the three Camp Scott, Kiowa Unit Counselors, was the second witness called during the preliminary trial.

Carla arrived at camp on Sunday, June 12th at around 12:30PM. She went to the Kiowa Unit and, like Dee Elder, noticed that a tent's flap had a six inch rip in it that had not been there when she left on Friday afternoon.

When the children arrived that Sunday, there was a mix-up and the Kiowa Unit had been assigned twenty-seven campers instead of twenty-eight. After the Kiowa Unit Campers picked out their bunkmates and tents, the counselors took them to the unit kitchen and played name games before dinner in order to get better-acquainted with each other. After dinner, when the campers were back in their units, the rain stopped around 8:00PM, and the Kiowa Unit counselors brought the Kiowa campers to the unit kitchen. They talked to the children and elected girls as camp representatives for the camp council, and then they opened the cookies and had one of the campers, Denise Milner, pass them out to the other campers.

After the campers were sent to bed, Carla visited the Arapaho Unit to spend time with some friends. At around 11:30PM, when Carla had returned to the Kiowa Unit and was getting ready for bed, some of the kids started giggling and laughing. Carla took her flashlight walked around the unit to tell the children in the tents to be quiet. She walked by tents 6 and 7 and heard no noise, so she continued on to the other tents. Carla returned to the Counselors' tent and went to sleep, only to be awakened again around 12:30am by all four girls from tent #1. They were in the latrine, and banging the door and the latrine lids, so Carla got up and met the four girls on their way back to their tent. Carla scolded them for making so much noise, and then helped them get back to their tent. Between 1 and 1:30AM, the children in tent #1 started giggling and woke Carla. At this time, she started hearing another sound from farther away, like it was near the back fence of the camp, which was across the road from the Kiowa Counselors' tent. Dee had also woken and heard the same noise, but neither counselor was able to identify the sound. They had never heard anything like it before, and thought it might be an animal. Carla got out of bed and told Dee she would go see what the noise was and then head over to tent #4. Carla then walked out on the trail and across the road to the fence. There, she pointed her flashlight toward the sound in a bushy area on the other side of the fence. The noise, which she described as sounding something like a fog horn, frog or a snore, stopped when the light was pointed in the area. She started to walk away when the noise started again, and she started back over to the fence once again before making the decision that it was an animal. She went back toward the tents and had told the girls in tent #4 to be quiet. She then walked down to tent 6 and 7 and went back to bed.

At 6:00AM Carla's wind-up alarm started ringing, so she collected her personal items and headed down the footpath to the road toward the Staff House to take a hot shower.

As Carla walked, she saw sleeping bags in the fork of the road. At first, she thought that these were more of the campers luggage that had been delivered late. She started in that direction in order to pick up the sleeping bags, and she planned to put them in the unit's kitchen for someone to claim. When she got closer, she saw it was more than just sleeping bags; it was also a little girl. Carla did not know who it was, or which unit she was from, but the little girl appeared dead. Carla could not grasp what had happened and ran back to the counselors' tent where she woke Dee and Susan and told them "they needed to count the kids because she had found a body in the road." Carla told Dee to "start with tent #7, and she would start at tent #1 and work their way through the unit." As Carla started to check tent 3, Dee ran over and told them "there's nobody in tent 7," and then said "there's blood." Carla then decided to check the rest of the tents hoping the kids had got scared and had gone to someone else's tent. Carla ran to tent #7 and looked in. First, she saw "blood on the corner of one of the mattresses and some stuff all over the floor, but there weren't any sleeping bags or children." Carla thought "maybe one of the kids started her period." Next, Carla told Dee and Susan to stay in the camp area and make sure none of the kids got out of their tents while she ran to get the camp nurse and Barbara Day.

Carla ran to the infirmary and told the nurse, Mary Ann Alaback, "There was a body down in Kiowa in the fork", and that she needed her to "get down there real fast." Carla then went to Barbara Day's office and woke her and her husband. The three went in the camp station wagon. When they arrived at the Kiowa area, nurse Mary Ann ran over to the car and informed them there were three bodies. Carla got out of the car and walked over to the bodies. She then realized it was the little Milner girl. Richard Day walked around the bodies, and Barbara announced that they needed to call the police. Barbara told Carla not to tell anyone, and for her to get the kids out of the Kiowa Unit quickly because the highway patrol would be coming. Carla was sure she needed help getting the rest of the kids out, so she ran to the Arapaho Unit to get her friend who was a counselor in training. Once the kids were up and had gathered at the unit's kitchen, Dee and Susan returned and helped get the girls out of the unit. Carla stayed at the Great Hall and never returned back to the Kiowa Unit that day. Later on that day, she was interviewed by law enforcement agents who wanted to know what had happened and what she had seen. At around 5:00PM, she left the camp to go home. On Tuesday, the 14th of June, she returned to Camp Scott where she was again interviewed by OSBI Agents and law enforcement personnel.

After the interviews, Carla went with the other two Kiowa Unit counselors to inventory and collect her personal belongings from the counselors' tent, where she found her second pair of glasses, the glasses' case and her capo were missing. On Wednesday the 15th of June she was asked to return to camp for more questioning, where three OSBI agents asked her about people at the camp, if there were any homosexuals at the camp. They then took Carla's hair blood, and saliva samples, and her fingerprints. The OSBI continued to stay in touch with Carla after that week and at various times contacted her with more questions.

During the witness testimony, Carla gave an account of an incident that occurred during the orientation week. She had hurt her back while lifting sailboats, and stayed in the Staff House one evening. That night, she heard noises behind the staff house, similar to someone scratching on, or rubbing against, the back screen. Carla yelled out and asked who was there. Nobody answered, and then she had heard someone walking away. Carla jumped up and looked out the front window. She thought it might have been Sally, the camp's dog, but she saw Sally running across the yard barking and growling at something Carla could not see.[164]

Susan Emery, called as a witness on June 12th, 1978.
Susan Emery was the third Kiowa Unit Counselor called as a witness during the preliminary trial.

Susan arrived at the camp on Sunday, June 12th at around noon with her fiancé Randy, who had driven her to the camp. Susan and Randy took a short hike down to Spring Creek and then returned to move her things into the Kiowa counselors' tent. Randy left before the campers arrived.

After dinner that night, the campers had started back toward the Kiowa Unit. Susan took one of the campers to the infirmary to get her medication and then escorted the child back to her tent. At around 9:00PM, Susan went to the staff house and returned to the Kiowa Unit at 10:00PM, where she went to bed. The next thing she remembered was Carla's alarm going off at 6:00AM, and Carla leaving the tent, only to return telling Dee that they had needed to count the girls. Susan got out of bed and went with Carla to tent #1 and checked to see if all the girls were there. Meanwhile, Dee headed to tent #7 to start counting. When Susan and Carla got to tent three, Dee came over and told them that the three girls were missing in tent#7. After checking tents 4, 5, and 6, all three counselors went to tent #7 and opened the tent flap. They saw no girls, but saw blood on the bed and floor. The first thing Susan thought was that one of the girls had started her period in the middle of the night, gotten scared and went to find the camp nurse. Carla then said something about there being sleeping bags in the road, so Susan went down the road where she saw one body. Stunned, Susan turned around, took a few steps and then screamed. Dee ran over to Susan and put her hand over her mouth and reminded her not to scare the other girls. Susan went back to the Counselors' tents where she put on her shoes and then headed back out on the road where the body was. There, she met up with Mary Ann, the camp nurse. She stayed there, and then Barbara and Richard Day showed up. Susan walked over to the zipped-up sleeping bags near the body and picked up one bag, and then the other. She realized there was something in the bags and immediately set them down.

Later on that day, when the children had left on the buses going back to Tulsa, Susan stayed at the camp for more interviews with officials until around 5:00PM.

Susan Emery was asked about the purse she brought with her to camp. On the night of June 12th, 1977 Susan had placed the purse under her cot in the counselors' tent directly under her head. Susan had seen the purse before she went to sleep, but on June 14th, when the Kiowa counselors' were allowed to go back into their tent to inventory and collect personal belongings, she realized her purse was missing. She described a pair of sunglasses and sunglasses case that was inside her purse among other items.

She was also asked about a towel that had been used at the counselors' tent the night of June the 12th during and after the rain storm. That first night, one of the counselors draped a towel over the edge of the tent, right in front of Carla Wilhite's bed. Susan saw the towel again on June 14th while they were collecting their personal belongings, and since she saw blood on the towel, it was left there and collected as evidence.

Sunglasses and the sunglasses case were both found at one of the caves and had been taken into evidence by law enforcement agents after the June 13th murders. This evidence was shown to Susan during the trial, and she positively identified them as being the ones that were in her purse.[167]

Barbara Day, called as a witness on June 8th, 1978.
Barbara Day was the Camp Director at Camp Scott in 1977. She arrived at Camp Scott on June the 5th and stayed at the Camp Director's Office with her husband Richard.

On June 12th, 1977, Barbara had been responsible for making sure all the staff and the children had arrived, and she made certain the campers were assigned and placed in their correct units. Barbara also checked to ensure the equipment necessary for each unit was in the correct locations. Each camp unit had walkie-talkies to be used for emergency communication. The base unit was located in the Camp Director's Office, but Barbara could not get the base unit to operate. So, a repairman had been scheduled to come to camp on Monday June 13th to get it working.

When the buses dropped the children off and left camp, and everyone was at their camp units, Barbara and her husband met back up and remained together during dinner at the Great Hall. They stayed there until approximately 7:30PM, when Barbara and Richard left for town to buy milk because they were out. When they got to the camp's front gate, they noticed a car parked outside the gate with four people inside. Neither she nor her husband stopped or talked to the people because they were not on camp property. Within an hour, Barbara and Richard returned to camp and the car was gone.

On the morning of June 13th, Barbara was awakened at 6:10AM by Carla Wilhite yelling and banging on the latched screen door of the Director's Office. Barbara and Richard both threw clothes on and jumped into the yellow station wagon with Carla, who drove down to the Kiowa camp and parked directly behind the Camp Nurse's car.

When Barbara got out of the car, she saw Susan Emery, Nurse Mary Ann Alaback and Dee Elder standing around, seemingly upset. Barbara asked them where the body was, and they pointed. Barbara approached what was on the side of the camp road, she then observed the presence of a young girl lying across a sleeping bag on the ground, without clothes from the waist down and legs spread far apart. The girl appeared to have been hit in the head and had dried blood on her forehead. Next to her body, on the ground, were two zipped up sleeping bags. Barbara suggested they cover the child's body to keep other campers from accidently seeing her, so Richard pulled the sleeping bag over the top of Milner's body.

Barbara focused in on the two sleeping bags that were zipped up and lying near the body. She asked how many other children were missing. Susan, who had been standing near the sleeping bags, leaned over and picked one up and then quickly dropped it, indicating there was something in the two zipped up sleeping bags. Richard then felt one of the bags without unzipping it and determined, by touch, that there were bodies or body parts in the bags. Barbara then left Nurse Alaback and one of the counselors there while she and Richard went to seek help.

Barbara and Richard drove up to the camp ranger's house where they woke Ben Woodward up and told him what had happened. Barbara instructed Ben and her husband, Richard, to take Ben's truck and return to the Kiowa location. There, they would give further assistance to the counselors to protect and secure the area so the counselors could be free to tend to the remaining children in the Kiowa Unit.

Barbara then went to her office and telephoned the Highway Patrol in Vinita. Oklahoma. She then phoned her Executive Director, Bonnie Brewster at her home and advised her on what had happened.

Barbara Day then rang the camp bell which was located directly in front of the Director's Office. Once she rang the bell she realized it was earlier than normal, so she jumped in her car and drove to each unit's staff tent. Barbara told the counselors that there had been an emergency in the camp, and all the children needed to be taken by the road only to the Great Hall for an early breakfast, and no trails should be used.

Barbara returned the car back to the Director's Office and walked back to the Kiowa Unit area where the bodies had been found. There, she was met by Highway Patrolman Harold Berry, Mayes County Sherriff Pete Weaver and Dr. Collins. Barbara led Sherriff Weaver, Officer Berry and Dr. Collins through the Kiowa Unit where they looked inside all the tents along the way to the victims' tent (#7). When they arrived at the victims' tent and opened the front flap, Barbara saw blood on a cot and blood on the floor underneath the cot. Three cots were missing the mattress covers, and the sleeping bags were gone. The blood on the floor had been smeared as though wiped up in an attempt to clean it. After Officer Berry and Sherriff Weaver began looking inside and around the tent, Barbara left the area.

Barbara then met with Bonnie Brewster and they returned to the Director's Office. They discussed whether to close the camp and worked on determining the exact identity of the victims. Barbara had to make plans of how the children would eat lunch, where they would go, and what they would do with 135 children until the buses arrived to pick them up.

Barbara was questioned on and off by the OSBI and other law enforcement personnel until Wednesday June 15th. She was given a formal interview, fingerprinted by the OSBI and re-reviewed the events of June 13th. She discussed the staff and their personal backgrounds and answered personal questions about her own life. After the interview, she stayed in constant contact with the OSBI throughout the summer of 1977. Barbara had no knowledge of any prowlers prior to the murders and had only heard of disturbances at the camp after the fact.

Barbara Day told how, in April 1977 at the Cadet Camporee Program held at camp Scott, she had been at the camp as an observer to see the camp in action while a large group of over 200 were there. She and her husband Richard spent the weekend observing the programs and had walked the units and had seen how everything worked. Barbara Homestead was the name of the volunteer who had been the Director of the Cadet Camporee. Barbara Day had not been informed of a threatening note which had been found by 16-year-old Michelle Hoffman, a Senior Scout assisting at the Cadet Camporee Program. After the murders occurred, Barbara Day was later contacted about the threatening note found during the Cadet Camporee.

Barbara Day had been present when an episode that was referred to as a "figment of a camper's imagination" happened, during the Camporee, where a child had gone into hysterics because she thought she saw a dummy hanging from a tree. When Barbara, Richard and the staff of the Cadet Camporee investigated, they found only tree limbs hanging strangely that possibly resembled an "effigy" hanging from a limb.[165]

Richard Day, called as a witness on June 26th, 1978.
Richard Day, husband of Barbara Day, had been acquainted with the camp because his mother served as Camp Director at Camp Scott some 40 years prior to 1977.

On Sunday afternoon, June the 12th, around 2 or 3pm, Richard went hiking. While walking down a trail, a couple of miles from the heart of the camp, he encountered a man with medium length dark hair, approximately six feet tall, and somewhat thin. The man was carrying a clear plastic jug. The stranger explained to Richard that he was after water from the creek. After talking to the man, Richard returned back to the main area of the camp and spent the rest of the evening with his wife Barbara.

The next morning, June 13th, Richard and his wife were summoned by Carla Wilhite to the Kiowa Unit area. Richard had medical training in the Navy as a surgical nurse. When he and his wife, Barbara, observed the crime scene he had saw a young girl lying unclothed, except for a shirt. He noticed she had blood and a wound on the right side of her head. He tried to check for a pulse but was unable to because something was around her neck, but it became apparent to him that she was deceased. He instructed the camp nurse to stay with the body while he and Barbara went to get Ben, the Ranger.

Later, at the Director's Office, Bonnie Brewster, the Girl Scout Director arrived and instructed Richard to wait at the Staff House in case some of the children's parents arrived. He was instructed to explain the situation and assure the parents that their daughters were not involved in the incident. He assisted in taking the buses down to "Wildcat Williams" swimming area to pick up the girls.

Richard Day was later interviewed and fingerprinted, and had hair samples taken. He was also given a Polygraph test.[171]

Ben Woodward, called as a witness on June 8th, 1978.
Ben Woodward was employed by the Magic Empire Council for three years and was the Camp Ranger. He lived at Camp Scott in the Ranger House with his wife and four children. At the camp, it was the Camp Ranger's responsibility to provide security by keeping trespassers out and locking the gate after 10:30pm.

On the 11th of June 1977, it was Ben's responsibility to check all the tents before the children arrived. During his inspection, he found in the Kiowa Unit that a brand new tent had a 5 foot piece of canvas cut off the front flap. He had searched the area to see if he could find the missing canvas piece and found nothing.

On the night of June 12th, at around 10:30PM, Ben drove to town to pick his sixteen year old daughter, Tammy, up from work at B and B Drive In. At about 10:45PM they arrived back at Camp Scott and locked the front gate. At that time, Ben did not see any cars parked or any unusual activity in the area of the camp.

The next morning at approximately 6:00AM, Ben was awakened by Barbara and Richard Day, who told him, "Three little girls had been murders down at the Kiowa Unit." Barbara used the Camp Ranger's house phone to call Highway Patrolman Berry, who lived only a half a mile from the camp.

Ben went to the scene of the crime while Richard Day took Ben's truck to unlock the front gate for Highway Patrolman Berry. As Ben looked around the scene he observed two sleeping bags which appeared to be on top of each other, and one little girl lying out in the open. She had a pajama top on, her hands were bound behind her, and it looked like she had been molested. He also observed a flashlight, a roll of tape and a strip of tape on the clothing around the waist of the body. In a few minutes, Trooper Berry arrived, followed by Sherriff Weaver. As others started arriving, the officers wanted the area roped off. Ben got a spool of nylon rope and placed it as directed by Sheriff Weaver. Later on in the day the OSBI asked Ben for a saw which he provided, and the OSBI used it to cut a piece of the floor out in the victims' tent.

The next day, June 14th, Ben was interviewed by the OSBI, who also taken his fingerprints, saliva and hair samples. Later, Ben was given a polygraph test.

Ben explained that the tent canvas had been setup before the orientation week in 1977. He had hired 3 people and it had taken 5 days to put up the tents in all the units at Camp Scott. When not in use, the tents were stored at each unit's kitchen closet area. Also stored in the unit's kitchen closets were rakes, shovels and lockers.[165]

Celia Stall, called as a witness on June 26, 1978

Celia Stall was the Assistant Unit Leader at the Quapaw Unit at Camp Scott in 1977. The week before the opening of the camp, (orientation week), Celia knew of two counselors named Sunny Doherty and Donna Dixon who had been followed. One night, after dark, someone followed them with a flashlight down the Cookie Trail Road to the Staff House, where they both hid under a car. At the end of the orientation week, Celia had a conversation with her friend Judy Hall, who told her about a man who had entered her tent. Judy had been sick and stayed in her tent alone. A man entered the back of the tent, so Judy had stayed very still and quiet. He had not bothered her, and she had never seen who it was.

During the first night of camp, June 12th, at around 1 or 2:00AM, Celia and the other two Quapaw counselors were awakened by screams or crying coming from the woods. All three left the tent and found a little girl wondering around and sleepwalking. They all went back to bed and at approximately 6:00AM the next morning Dee Elder showed up at the counselors' tent. She was crying, and had woken Linda Henderson. Dee took Linda away and told her something, and then the two went around and checked all the tents together. Linda returned to the tent and told Celia and Kathy Elder what had happened.

Later on Monday, June 13th, while the Quapaw Counselors were getting the Quapaw campers dressed and packed up to leave, Kathy Elder was helping some of the girls pack. The girls began telling Kathy and Celia about how they had seen a couple of men. They had been wearing army boots and khaki pants behind their tents, tent 3, and one of the men had been seen over by the latrine. The 4 campers did not see the faces of any of the men because it was too dark, but they heard the men's voices and saw their legs and feet from looking out the bottom of their tent. The campers told Kathy and Celia they had been so scared they all jumped into one sleeping bag and stayed that way the rest of the night.[171]

117

Trooper Harold Berry, called as a witness on June 8th, 1978.
Highway Patrol Trooper Harold Berry received a phone call from
his District Headquarters to go to Camp Scott on June 13th, 1977.
He arrived at Camp Scott at approximately 6:40AM, and was met
by Richard Day at the camp's front gate. Richard led him to the
victim's bodies. Trooper Berry pulled his patrol car up to the
scene, got out and walked over to where the bodies were.. He
visually looked around the bodies and went back to his car's unit
radio where he called his headquarters and requested that the
Sheriff of Mayes County be notified. He was then advised that the
Sheriff was en-route to the scene. Trooper Berry then notified the
Locust Grove Police Department for assistance in securing the
scene of the crime. He asked the camp personnel standing around
him not to allow anyone into the area.

Trooper Berry then described that he saw a body partially covered
by a sleeping bag. He also saw a roll of black duct tape and a
flashlight nearby.

Twenty-five minutes after Trooper Berry arrived at the scene,
Sheriff Weaver and Dr. Collins arrived. Once the Sheriff and
Doctor viewed the scene where the bodies were located, Barbara
Day took the Sheriff, Dr. Collins, and Trooper Berry to the
victims' tent. When they had arrived at the tent Trooper Berry
glanced inside the tent and observed dried blood on the floor. At
the back of the tent, Trooper Berry observed a tear or slit in the

tent's back canvas, and it appeared to him that this might have been how the intruder or intruders gained entrance into the tent. After they looked inside and walked around the tent, they returned to where the bodies were located.

Trooper Berry went to the Camp Director's office and phoned his District Headquarters to speak to his superiors at Vinita, Oklahoma and advise them as to what had happened.

After Barbara Day told Trooper Berry the names of the three victims, Berry devised a plan. Trooper Berry had the Kiowa Counselors ask the remaining Kiowa Unit campers if they had heard or seen anything during the night since none of the campers had been told about the murders. Berry instructed Dee Elder, Carla Wilhite and Susan Emery to make up a story about the camp lantern being stolen, and ask if any of the little girls had seen or heard anything. None of the children had seen or heard anything.

Trooper Berry helped search the Kiowa Unit area for any evidence on the 13th, and in the following days he stood by and assisted in various other tasks as needed by his superiors at the camp for approximately eight to nine additional days.

The only other time Trooper Berry had been called to Camp Scott was four to five years earlier when he took a report due to several tents being stolen.[165]

119

Gene 'Pete' Weaver, called as a witness on June 27th, 1978. Gene Weaver was the Sheriff of Mayes County in 1977, and was the second officer to arrive at Camp Scott on June 13th, 1977.

Upon his arrival, Trooper Harold Berry was already at the scene. Weaver walked to the crime scene and observed the sleeping bags and the exposed body. He reached down and touched the arm of the victim and approximated her body temperature at around 70 degrees. He observed the red and white sportsman flashlight which had a green plastic taped over the lens with a small hole torn in it. He observed the black roll of duct tape leaning across the tree two feet from the body. Weaver radioed the OSBI to send agents and technicians to assist in the processing of the crime scene.

At some point, Weaver went to look inside the victims' tent where he noticed a child's blue and white tennis shoe on the tent's wooden floor and blood on the two left bunks in the tent. He also noticed the smeared blood on the floor with what appeared to be two shoe prints in the blood. One print looked to be a military-type tread with heavy lugs on the sole, and the other was a smaller shoe print, approximately a size seven, with round, suction-type tread. Both prints appeared to be placed there after the clean-up operation. In a later search of the area, Weaver and a deputy crawled on hands and knees up the trail between the Kiowa Unit and Arapaho Unit, which was a distance of 150 to 200 yards beyond Kiowa Unit. They observed the same military-type footprint traveling in the direction of the Kiowa unit. The footprint appeared to be a ten or eleven in size. Weaver went around the outside of the victims' tent and observed that at the rear northwest corner the tent flap had been unhooked, and short hair was stuck in the canvas fabric.

Weaver assisted in coordinating the investigation and processing the scene. A thorough search of the area was started near the area where the bodies were located and passed by the Kiowa Unit fire ring and around the kitchen unit towards the victims' tent.

Early on, Weaver had to make a decision on whether or not to call for tracking dogs. He decided it was more valuable to protect and process the scene for physical evidence. He would later use the help and rely on dogs for tracking. On or around the 15[th,] tracking dogs were brought in from Pennsylvania. Their search started near the area where the victims' bodies had been found in the Kiowa area. Weaver observed the dogs as they proceeded from the starting location to tent 7, which was the victims' tent. The dogs then sat down on the wooden platform step. The dogs were taken behind the tent, scented and headed towards the Arapaho Unit area through the back foot trails. The dogs then headed east down another path towards the Cookie Trail Road and they then followed the Cookie Trail Road out through Camp Scott's front gate. They almost reached Highway 82 when they turned left on a county road. The dogs went to the intersection of Twin Bridge Road and traveled in a southerly direction on Earbob Road to the gate of the Shroff residences where they went to the front porch and sat down.[172]

Carey Thurman, called as a witness on June 28th, 1978
Carey Thurman was an Agent with the Oklahoma State Bureau of Investigation and was the first OSBI agent at the crime scene. He would later be assigned as the Case Agent.

When Agent Mike Wilkerson arrived, he and Carey Thurman took measurements of the crime scene. They were joined by other Agents and proceeded to take photographs of the bodies as well as anything that they thought might be evidence lying near the bodies and in the Kiowa Camp area. Thurman also assisted in inventorying the personal effects from the victims' tent (tent #7).

During the trial, Carey Thurman was asked about a crowbar being found. Thurman said he was not the person who found the crowbar, but it had been found lying along the southern edge of the camp, adjacent to the Kiowa Camp area. It was almost underneath the barbed wire fence. The crowbar had been collected and processed and had been found negative for human blood and negative as being an instrument used to enter the Shroff's residence. Thurman also had a number of hatchets submitted, and two of the hatchets he remembered because one had a yellow handle and had been found in one of the other camp units and the other had been in a leather case he had received from Sheriff

Weaver. Both hatchets had been processed and were negative for human blood.

Carey Thurman was asked if the boot print found at Camp Scott seemed to be the same type as the ones seen at cave #2, Shroff's residence and the grocery store that had been burglarized. All the prints appeared to be the same.[173]

David Parker, called as a witness on June 8th, 1978.
David Parker lived in Pryor Oklahoma and was employed part-time for Jim Green's Funeral Home as an ambulance driver.

On June 13[th,] Parker received a call for assistance. David and his father Paul Parker drove to Locust Grove and were instructed via radio to meet up with, and follow the Sheriff. At approximately 7:00 AM, Sheriff Weaver led them into Camp Scott and parked near the Kiowa Unit Camp. David hen met with another ambulance driver from Jim Green's Funeral home, Rick Stevens. Stevens had driven another ambulance to the site. They stood around for some time and then were asked to assist in a search of the area. The search started at the road closest to the victims' bodies and traveled through the Kiowa camp area.

In all, three ambulances arrived at the scene that morning: two from Jim Greens Funeral home and one from Wilson-Cunningham ambulance. By early afternoon, the OSBI gave instructions to remove the victims' bodies and take them to the Medical Examiner's office in Tulsa, Oklahoma. Rick Stevens and David Parker loaded all three little girls' bodies into Rick Stevens' ambulance, and both men transported the victims to Tulsa Oklahoma.[165]

Beverly Hough, called as a witness on June 28th, 1978

Beverly Hough was an Investigator for the Office of the District Attorney. She interviewed Dee Elder, Carla Wilhite and Susan Emery on June 13th as well as some of the Kiowa youngsters. Beverly was present when the three Kiowa Unit counselors' were brought back to Camp Scott on the 14th for a more in-depth interview with the OSBI. After the interviews were completed, the three counselors were allowed back to the Kiowa Unit to collect their personal items from their tent. Beverly was present while the counselors inventoried and collected their things. Beverly observed a towel draped over the front step of the counselors' tent. The towel appeared to have blood smeared on it, so Beverly called this to the attention of the OSBI Agents. The towel was Susan Emery's, and it had a small smear of blood on it, as though something had brushed lightly against it. The towel had been near Carla Wilhite's orange crate which was right inside the front of the tent. The crate was where Carla kept one of her pair of glasses. These were the glasses Carla was missing, and which were found by investigators off the Kiowa trail area. The counselors had no idea how or why there was blood on the towel.[173]

Dr. Neal Hoffman, called as a witness on June 9th, 1978.

Dr. Hoffman was the Forensic Pathologist and the Assistant Chief Medical Examiner for the State of Oklahoma. Dr. Hoffman performed the autopsies on all three victims. The following individuals were present at the autopsies: Gary Jenson, John Rolf, Linda Mills, Janice Davis, Dennis Reimer and several other officials.

Dr. Hoffman started the autopsy procedures sometime after 3:30PM on June 13th, 1977. Case numbers had been assigned. Next, he examined the external covers over the bodies for any possibility of trace evidence. Then, the bodies were fumed with iodine vapor to detect any latent fingerprints. Photographs were taken, and the bodies were moved to the autopsy table where further external and internal examinations were carried out. Cotton tipped swabs, clothing, hair samples, nail clippings, and any other items found in the sleeping bags were handed over to Janice Davis and Dennis Reimer of the OSBI. Each autopsy was performed separately, starting with the Milner girl. Guse was second and Farmer was third. Six swabs, in groups of two, were used to collect evidence from the mouth, anus and vagina of each child.

Both Milner and Guse had cording tied around parts of their bodies. Milner had a type of black adhesive tape, such as bookbinding or duct tape, across the front chest of the garment, and also had the black tape wrapped around her wrists.

Milner had a portion of a terry cloth like material under her chin, and it had been adjoined to an elastic ribbed cloth material, similar to an ace bandage that might have been used as a gag. Farmer did not have any ties or ligatures on or around her body.

- Doris Denise Milner: probable cause of death - asphyxiation due to ligature strangulation.
- Michelle Guse: probable cause of death - blunt trauma to the head
- Lori Lee Farmer: probable cause of death - blunt trauma to the head.

All three deaths occurred between 2:00AM and 6:00AM.[166]

Arthur Linville, called as a witness on June 9 and June 12, 1978
Linville was an Agent with the Oklahoma State Bureau of Investigations. He flew from Chickasha, Oklahoma to Oklahoma City on the morning of June 13th and picked up two OSBI technicians, Paul Esquinaldo and Larry Mullins. They then flew to Pryor, Oklahoma where they were picked up by Highway Patrolman, Charlie Newton. Newton drove them south of Locust Grove, Oklahoma to Camp Scott. Linville was in charge of overseeing the collection of evidence and also the preservation of the crime scene and the surrounding area.

On June 13th Linville took into custody the following pieces of evidence:

- A pair of eyeglasses that was found seven feet from the road leading into the Kiowa camp.

- A guitar capo located two feet from the glasses

- A red glasses case with gold trim located five feet north of the road leading into the Kiowa camp.

- A girl's hairpiece with two blue balls attached to it located 108 feet east from the opening of the victims' tent.

- A large roll of black duct tape which had been found leaning against a tree near the bodies.

- A red flashlight with masking tape and green plastic over the lens located near the tree where the bodies were located

- A piece of black duct tape laying on the ground near where the red flashlight had been collected.

All the items of evidence were photographed before being collected.

Next, Linville's team processed the tent. Photographs were taken outside of the tent. The tent was then opened, and photographs were taken from the outside looking inside. Photographs of the bloody footprints were taken, and then the cots were removed to the outside of the tent. All of the items belonging to the girls was inventoried and removed.

The inside of the tent was examined and numerous hairs, fiber and materials found on the floor were picked up, packaged and labeled. The floor of the tent was vacuumed with a crime scene vacuum cleaner which contained elaborate system of filters.

Next, sections of the tent's wooden floor with the bloody footprints were cut out using a hand saw and chainsaw to preserve the footprint evidence. Linville described the boot footprints as a waffle-type pattern similar to, but not exactly like a jungle or military boot.

Linville retained all the items of evidence, including the sections of the floor, and loaded them into an aircraft, which was flown to the Oklahoma City Office of the Oklahoma State Bureau of Investigation. The evidence was submitted the evidence to the OSBI Identification Section laboratory.

Linville was again asked to the witness stand on June 12th, 1978, where he talked about additional evidence, including information about finding a newspaper at a cave that matched with the newspaper that had been found in the battery compartment of the red flashlight found near the victims' bodies. Also found at the cave was a roll of masking tape with a piece of green plastic stuck to the edge of the tape. This had a general consistency to the tape and green plastic that was covering the lens of the red flashlight.

Linville was also asked about evidence found at another location on Camp Scott's property just southwest of the Kiowa Unit tents. Along the fence line between Camp Scott and John Cavalier's property, evidence had been found that included a piece of plastic, three Pabst Blue Ribbon beer bottles and a crowbar. These items were found by law enforcement on June 13th, 1977. All the evidence had been tested for fingerprints, and none were found on any of the items.[166]

Larry Mullins, called as a witness on June 9th, 1978.
Larry Mullins was the fingerprint technician for the OSBI, and he assisted Arthur Linville at Camp Scott on June 13th, 1977. Once all the evidence had been collected and flown to the lab in Oklahoma City, Larry Mullins took the red flashlight apart and found a piece of newspaper under the battery. The newspaper was processed for latent fingerprints, but none were found. There was a partial latent fingerprint lifted from the reflector of the flashlight, but no fingerprints were found on the body of the flashlight or the battery inside.

When Mullins inspected tent #7, the victims' personal items and the cots had been removed from inside the tent. The metal frames were processed for latent fingerprints by Mullins, who had found a single latent print on one of the cots. Neither the fingerprint on the flashlight, nor the fingerprint found on the cot was linked to anyone.[166]

Paul D. Boyd, called as a witness on June 9th, 1978

Paul Boyd was the Chief Identification Officer for the Oklahoma State Bureau of Investigation and on June 13th, 1977, Boyd assisted in the examination of evidence taken from the three victims' bodies during the autopsies at the Medical Examiner's Office in Tulsa, Oklahoma. During the autopsy of Milner, he was handed the pajama top which had been removed from her body. Attached to the front of the pajama top was a strip of black duct tape and a piece of a three-strand spiral cotton cord. He was then handed the gag that had been around Milner's neck, which he described as a rolled terry cloth towel which was stitched closed by green thread and a cord going through the center of the towel.

During his examination of the black tape on June 14th at the OSBI lab in Oklahoma City, he found three hairs attached to the inner surface of the tape. He also received more tape and cord that had been removed from around Milner's wrists. When they were examined, he concluded the cord had been placed around the wrist first, and the tape had been wrapped over the cord. The only fingerprint found on the tape from around the wrist was from Milner herself.[166]

Dennis Reimer, called as a witness on June 13th, 1978.

Dennis Reimer was a Forensic Chemist for the OSBI, and on June 13th, 1977, Reimer assisted in the examination of evidence taken from the three victims at the Medical Examiner's Office in Tulsa Oklahoma. He was given the blood samples from all three victims, as well as the swabs and the smears that were made from the swabs used by Dr. Hoffman. The swabs were tested to determine if male seminal fluid was present, and the following results were found: Milner's oral and anus swabs were negative, but the vaginal swab tested positive for seminal fluid; Oral and vaginal swabs from Guse were negative, but the anal swab showed a positive result for seminal fluid.; and all swabs taken from Farmer were negative for any seminal fluid.[166]

Janice Davis, called as a witness on June 13th, 1978
Janice Davis' role was to analyze substances brought into the OSBI by law enforcement agencies. She dealt with criminal matters rather than civil matters.

Janice Davis was present for the autopsies conducted on all three victims, she determined the smear slide swabs taken at the Medical Examiner's office contained what appeared to be decomposed sperm from the following: Guse's anal swab slide, Milner's anal swab slide and also from Farmer's vaginal swab slide. Davis was also present when hair samples, blood samples and saliva samples were taken from Gene Hart at the Grand Valley Hospital in Pryor Oklahoma on April 18, 1978. Gene Hart's saliva showed him to be a secretor of blood group substance "O." Davis was questioned about the ability to utilize a stain from fluids such as semen, saliva or blood in order to positively identifying a person, to which she replied "no."[168]

Ann G. Reed, called as a witness on June 13th, 1978

Ann Reed was a forensic chemist for the OSBI dealt in serology and trace examinations, with particular focus in hair comparison. On July 5th, 1977 she began analysis on the hair that had been found on the tape removed from Milner's hands. The three sections of hair were dark, with mostly mongoloid characteristics as well as some Caucasian characteristics. There was also one hair found on Milner's pajama top that showed mongoloid characteristics with some Caucasian characteristics and was not from the scalp of Milner. The sweeping that had been done on the victims' tent floor revealed four pieces of hair that were dark and mongoloid with a slight Caucasian characteristic. However, there was also a hair that showed Caucasian characteristics without mongoloid characteristics, and it was determined this had probably come from the victims. At the time, there was no scientific method of identifying a person from a hair sample. The analysis relied solely on similarities. [168]

John Gosser, called as a witness on June 29th, 1978

John Gosser was present during the crime scene investigation and took soil samples as evidence around the area where the bodies were found. He was present when the dog handler used a semen sample to scent the dogs, and gathered samples from any area where Authorities noticed the dogs honing in. He was unaware of the soil samples' test.

Gosser was also on-site at the crime scene of the burglary of Sam's Corner grocery store. This burglary occurred during the same time-frame as the Camp Scott Murders. He took photographs of the crime scene and attempted to lift latent prints.[174]

Ernest Small, called as a witness on June 30th, 1978

Ernest Small was an Examiner of Question Documents and had examined the handwritten message on the cave 1 wall, which was located on Jack Shroff's property. This property was located near Camp Scott's property. Smith examined the writing and found it had been made with a black felt tip marker pen that had a tip of a width of 8/64th of an inch wide. Taking into consideration the writing instrument and writing surface (the cave wall), he would have possibly been unable to give a definite opinion on who wrote the message.[175]

David Hybarger, called as a witness on June 30th, 1978

On June 13, 1977, David Hybarger was employed by the State Medical Examiner's Office as a Field Agent. He was present during all three autopsies. He used a black light on all three victims' bodies, on all the clothing and all three sleeping bags. Test results were negative for the presence of seminal fluid. [175]

Gary Jensen, called as a witness on June 30th, 1978

Gary Jensen was employed by the State Medical Examiner's Office in 1977 as Chief Field Agent and was present at the autopsies of all three girls. He performed the iodine and silver plate method test in an attempt to find latent fingerprints on the bodies of the victims. He found a fingerprint that was considered "classifiable" but later, found that it was not.

Jensen was also present when the ultraviolet 'black light' process was used on the victims' bodies. The light detected something on the side of the victims' body which glowed fluorescent under the black light. The area of skin that glowed fluorescent appeared to possibly be the edge of an object such as the edge of a shoe print, but the attempts to photograph the impression were not successful.[175]

Larry Mullins, called as a witness on June 30th, 1978

Larry Mullins, Agent for the OSBI, testified that while investigating the robbery at Jack Shroff's residence, no latent fingerprints were found on the back door. Two fingerprints were found on the sliding patio door, one of which was the fingerprint of the homeowner, Jack Shroff. The second fingerprint was not identified, and had been checked against a list of suspects that returned no matches. They processed several other items inside the house for latent prints but found none.

Larry Mullins was also asked about the latent fingerprint found on the body of one of the victims. He identified the fingerprint as belonging to a Midwest Police Dispatcher who had accidently touched the silver plate prior to application to the girl's body. This plate had then transferred his fingerprint to the victim's skin. [175]

Ronald Clodfelter, called as a witness on June 30th, 1978
Ronald Clodfelter was an OSBI Agent in the Serology Trace Evidence section of the OSBI lab. He examined the cotton cord which had been removed from around Milner's body and wrists, as well as those removed from Guse's wrists. The cord had a measurement of three-eighths of an inch in thickness, and appeared to be the same cord used on both victims. When the cord was compared against samples of other rope and cord taken from various areas of Camp Scott, no similar cord was found. [175]

Jack Shroff, called as a witness on July 3rd, 1978
Jack Shroff was the owner of the ranch near Camp Scott that had been burglarized sometime after 3pm on the same night of the Girl Scout murders' at Camp Scott.

Shroff left his ranch on Sunday June 12th, 1977 after 3pm and had been in Tulsa, Oklahoma until the following day, June 13th when he returned around 3:00PM to discover he had been robbed. He noticed that his door had been pried open, and he was missing two six-packs of Pabst Blue Ribbon beer bottles. He repaired the door the burglar had used to gain entry, and later, while listening to the radio, heard about the murder of the girl scouts. He picked up the phone and reported the robbery to the Sheriff's department before returning to Tulsa around 6:00PM.

Shroff received several calls from the authorities, and returned to his ranch south of Locust Grove, Oklahoma around 10:00PM. Upon arrival, the Sheriff and several other people were there. They asked Mr. Shroff to go through his house to see what had been taken. He noted beer, food, meat, Bama pies, petroleum resistant black duct tape and a straw hat.. He gave the Sheriff a sample of his 3/8's nylon rope which he kept around the ranch. He also noted that someone had built a fire near one of his ponds.

As evidence, the OSBI wanted the door that had been pried upon from Shroff's house, so he cut out part of the door and door jam for them.

Jack Shroff had several close calls with the press and some law enforcement who thought he had been involved in the crime. However, the OSBI had taken Jack Shroff's fingerprints and had given him a polygraph test, and he was ruled out as a suspect.

Shroff testified that the FBI had been to his ranch and had wanted to sketch a picture of all the caves and terrain. He reported seeing strangers off and on near, or on, his property fishing in his fishing hole that had been stocked with fish, and that these strangers had been stealing his fish.

Shroff had had several firearms in his house, but they had not been disturbed.

Neither Jack, nor his son David, knew that the cave on their property was the one with the handwritten note on the cave's wall until sometime in June 1978.[176]

TYPICAL DESIGN OF A WOODEN PLATFORM TENT

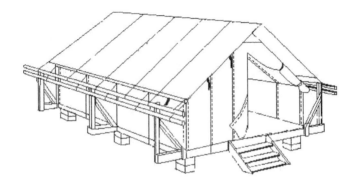

Camp Scott tents were 14x12 wooden platforms with a canvas shell.

12

INDIVIDUALS MENTIONED THROUGHOUT THE INVESTIGATION

Camp Scott leaders, Counselors and Workers

- **Nurse Mary Ann Alaback,** on-site camp nurse at Camp Scott in 1977.

- **Constance Cunningham**, Former Head counselor in early 70's at Camp Scott. Testified at the 1985 lawsuit trial about intruders at camp.

- **Barbara Day**, 1st year Camp Director for Camp Scott, who also testified during the preliminary hearing and the trial.

- **Dee Ann Elder,** One of the three camp counselors in the Kiowa unit where the girls were killed. Was the first counselor to open tent flap of the slain girls, and found nothing but blood.

- **Helen "Smitty" Gray**, former camp director in the early 1970's and testified at the 1985 trial.

- **Michelle Hoffman**, a senior Girl Scout who attended Camp Scott and found a threatening note in April 1977.

- **Barbara Homestead**, Coordinator of the spring Camporee at Camp Scott during which a threatening note was found in April 1977. Olmstead threw the note away.

- **Sally,** Camp Scotts full time Dog.

- **June Scoggins**, witness who testified she reported seeing a man enter a tent at night during a troop Campout in August 1975 at Camp Scott and had told Gray and other Magic Empire officials.

- **Celia Stall,** Quapaw Assistant Unit leader at Camp Scott, who testified that campers told her they saw men in the camp night of murders and days before the murders.

- **Carla Wilhite,** a Kiowa encampment counselor who found the murdered girls on the morning of June 13th, 1977.

- **Ben Woodward,** Camp Ranger at Camp Scott before and during the murders. After the murders, the land was guarded by camp ranger R.A. Martin and wife until it was sold.

Girl Scout / Magic Empire Council

- **Bonnie Brewster,** Executive director of Tulsa based Magic Empire Council of Girl Scouts from October 1974 to December 1997.

- **Frances Hesselbein**, Executive director of the Girl Scouts, U.S.A. National Council.
- **Nancy McDonald,** President of the board of directors of the Girl Scouts' Magic Empire Council.
- **Dan Rogers**, Attorney for the Magic Empire Council.
- **Ginny Young,** Public relations Director for Magic Empire Council.

OSBI - Oklahoma State Bureau of Investigation

- **Paul D. Boyd,** Chief Identification Officer for the OSBI.
- **Ronald Clodfelter,** OSBI Agent in the Serology Trace Evidence Section.
- **Janice Davis,** Forensic Chemist for the OSBI in 1977.
- **Tom Jordan,** OSBI Lab Technician.
- **Jeff Laird**, OSBI Director.
- **Ted Lempke**, Regional director and State investigator.
- **Arthur Linville,** OSBI Agent, In charge of overseeing the collection of evidence and preservation of the Crime Scene.
- **Larry Mullins,** Crime Scene Technician for the OSBI and State fingerprint expert.
- **Harvey Pratt**, OSBI Special Agent forensic artist.
- **Ann G. Reed**, Forensic Chemist for the OSBI in 1977.
- **Dennis Reimer,** Forensic Chemist for the OSBI.

- **Don Sharp,** Deputy Inspector of Special Investigations for OSBI.

- **Cary Thurman,** Regional OSBI agent, designated case agent, took crime scene photos at Camp Scott, interviewed camp Scott counselors.

- **Dick Wilkerson,** Deputy Director of the OSBI and Chief Inspector on the case.

- **Michael "Mike" Wilkerson,** Brother of Dick Wilkerson, Co-wrote 'Someone Cry for the Children,' inspector for the OSBI.

OHP = Oklahoma Highway Patrol

- **Harold Berry,** Highway Patrolman, who was the first officer on the scene.

- **Trooper Roger Osborn,** Highway Trooper.

- **Lt. Kenneth W. Vanhoy,** Director of Information for the Oklahoma Highway Patrol.

CSD = County Sheriff's Department

- **Al Boyer,** Undersheriff of Mayes County in 1977

- **Hugh Horton,** Mayes County Deputy Sheriff in 1977.

- **H.W. "Chief" Jordan,** Mayes County Sheriff in 1985.

- **Paul Smith,** Locust Grove deputy in 1977. Became Mayes County Sheriff in 1980.

- **Glen 'Pete' Weaver,** Mayes County Sheriff in 1977.

Locust Grove Police

- **Kenneth Decamp,** Locust Grove Police Chief in 1977.

Others

- **David Boren,** Governor of Oklahoma in 1977.
- **Judge Jess B. Clanton,** Special District Judge, who ordered Gene Hart to stand trial for the murders.
- **Richard Day,** Camp Scott Director Barbara Days husband.
- **S.M. Fallis Jr.,** Tulsa County District Attorney.
- **Ron Grimsley,** Pryor news reporter.
- **Gene Leroy Hart,** Only person charged with the murders, later found innocent in a court of law.
- **Royce Hobbs,** Mayes County Prosecutor in 1977
- **Dr. Neil Hoffman,** State Medical Examiner from Tulsa, performed the official autopsies.
- **Dr. Fred Jordan,** Medical Examiner, who performed the autopsy on Gene Hart.
- **Don Larken,** Trainer of the 3 dogs flown in with the owner from Pennsylvania.
- **Ted LaTurner,** private investigator in 1977 who had three suspects and filed a petition.

- **Gerald Manley**, Minister, who claimed to have known who committed the murders.

- **Dr. Robert Phillips**, Clinical psychologist, staff member of the statewide Barkours Foundation that diagnoses criminals for the court; profiled the killer at Camp Scott.

- **Garvin Isaac and Gary Pitchlynn**, Gene Hart's attorneys.

- **John Preston**, Pennsylvania State Policeman. Flown in with three tracking dogs from Pennsylvania, two shepherds and one Rottweiler. Harras, a shepherd dog, was a supposed wonder dog in tracking. The Rottweiler was good at tracking along roads, asphalt, blacktop and the second shepherd was a backup.

- **Dennis Reimer,** State Chemist from Tahlequah, analyzed clothing and other evidence.

- **Charles Sasser**, Author whose Girl Scouts Murder book was never published.

- **Jack Shroff**, Owner of farmhouse, close to Camp Scott, burglarized before the murders.

- **Dr. Vernon Sisney,** Well-known psychologist who profiled suspects in the killings.

- **William "Bill" Alton Stevens**, Kansas prisoner who was fingered as having been involved in the murders, and denied any involvement.

- **Sid Wise,** Mayes County District Attorney in 1977.

TIMELINE OF EVENTS THE NIGHT OF JUNE 12TH, 1977

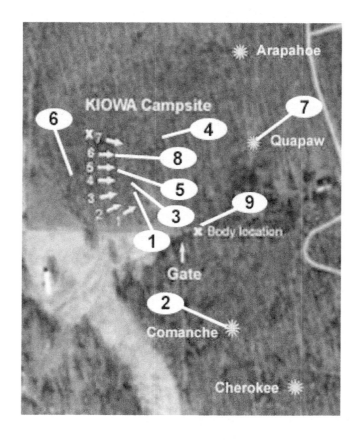

1. June 12th, 1977, before scouts arrived: Kiowa Counselor notices flap cut off tent at Kiowa campsite.[164]

2. Between 8 and 10pm: Comanche Unit Counselor sees a dim light heading towards Kiowa Unit encampment.[160]

3. 10pm: Dee makes tent checks of all tents at Kiowa unit.[164]

4. June 13th, 12:30am: Carla is awakened by campers laughing in latrine, went and escorted girls back to their tent, tent #1.[164]

5. 1:30am: Carla and Dee are awakened by girls giggling in tent #4. Carla heads toward the tent, and then hears a guttural moaning noise in the distance. Carla starts to investigate the noise but becomes scared and returns to bed.[164]

6. Dim light appears in the area of the Kiowa Unit.[160]

7. 2am at the Quapaw unit: A scout hears someone scream, "Momma".[160]

8. During the night at the Kiowa unit at Tent #6: A scout sees a light approach her tent, then flood the tent with light. A figure stared into the tent, then walked away.[160]

9. 6am: Carla finds the bodies.[164]

13

FREQUENTLY ASKED QUESTIONS

Why is the victims' tent sometimes called tent # 8 and other times called tent # 7?

Answer: The girl scouts who attended Camp Scott and stayed in the Kiowa Unit Campsite did not count the counselors tent as tent # 1. There were 7 scouts tents and 1 counselor's tent, but the police and investigators saw a total of 8 tents, and considered the "victims' tent" as tent # 8.

Are the victims' parents still living?

Answer: All the parents, as of 2014, are still living except for Walter Milner, Doris' father who passed away in 1997.

Do the victims' parents still want to know what happened?

Answer: Dr. Charles and Sheri Farmer actively speak to people about the case and still want the answer of who killed their daughter. Sheri promised her daughter, while visiting her grave in 1979, that she would not stop searching.

Who was Gene Leroy Hart and why isn't more written about him in your research?

Answer: Gene Hart was the sole person to be tried for the murders of the 3 little girls. A lot of information can be found about him in print and on the web. There are 2 sources I highly recommend, for finding out everything about Hart. www.girlscoutmurders.com and the 2011 book by my friend, Gloyd McCoy "Tent Number Eight". This book is a well-documented account of the trial and evidence brought forth regarding the Girl Scout murders and the acquittal of Gene Hart.

So who was the killer?

Answer: My research goes over details of different newspaper and media articles about the case. It is not my intent to push any one theory on who committed the crimes.

Can anyone go walk around the old Girl Scout, Camp Scott land?

Answer: The land is not public property; it is private property where people live. The owner 'does not' want people just showing up and walking around on their land. There are private property signs posted!

14

UNOFFICIAL

CRIME SCENE INFORMATION GLEANED

FROM MEDIA SOURCES:

CRIME SCENE INFORMATION		
OFFENSE: **Homicide**	DATE: **June 13th, 1977**	
LOCATION: **Camp Scott, Girl Scout Camp**		
CITY: **Locust Grove**	COUNTY: **Mayes**	STATE: **OK**

TIME NOTIFIED: **6am**		
NOTIFIED BY: **Barbara Day**	Camp Director	
OFFICER IN CHARGE: **Sheriff Glen "Pete" Weaver**	DEPT: **Mayes County Sheriff**	
FIRST OFFICER AT SCENE: **Harold Berry**	DEPT: **Oklahoma Highway**	

CIVILIANS WHO ENTERED THE CRIME SCENE	
NAME	DEPARTMENT
Carla Wilhite	Kiowa unit counselor
Dee Elder	Kiowa Unit Leader
Susan Emery	Kiowa unit counselor
Ben Woodward	Camp Ranger
Mary Alabeck	Camp Nurse
Barbara Day	Camp Director
Richard Day	Husband of camp director Barbara day

CRIME SCENE	
OFFENSE: **Homicide**	
LOCATION: **Camp Scott, Kiowa encampment**	
PERSON IN CHARGE: **Sheriff Glen "Pete" Weaver**	DEPT.: **Mayes County Sheriff**
PHOTOGRAPHER: **Cary Thurman**	DEPT.: **OSBI**

OFFICERS ASSISTING / SPECIALIST ON SCENE MORNING OF JUNE 13, 1977		
NAME	DEPARTMENT	ASSIGNMENT
Glen 'Pete' Weaver	Mayes County Sheriff	Lead
Harold Berry	Highway Patrolman	First on the scene
Cary Thurman	OSBI	Photographer
Arthur Lindville	OSBI	Processed evidence

WEATHER CONDITIONS @ 6am		
SCENE TEMP: **71.1**	OUTSIDE TEMP: **71.1 F**	SKY: **Overcast/Mostly**
WIND DIRECTION: **South**	WIND SPEED: **4.6**	PRECIPITATION: **0 @ 6am**
HUMIDITY: **87%**		

VICTIMS BODIES SENT TO

Tulsa Oklahoma State Medical Examiners Office

INFORMATION OF 1st DECEASED

LAST: Farmer	FIRST: Lori	MIDDLE: Lee
	CITY: Tulsa	STATE: OK

AGE: 8	RACE: White	SEX: Female	HAIR COLOR: Blonde	D.O.B.: 6/18/68

INFORMATION OF 2nd DECEASED

LAST: Milner	FIRST: Doris	MIDDLE: Denise
	CITY: Tulsa	STATE: OK

AGE: 10	RACE: Black	SEX: Female	HAIR COLOR: Black	D.O.B.: 2/05/67

INFORMATION OF 3rd DECEASED

LAST: Guse	FIRST: Michele	MIDDLE: Heather
	CITY: Broken Arrow	STATE: OK

AGE: 9	RACE: White	SEX: Female	HAIR COLOR: Brown	D.O.B.: 7/22/67

DECEASED FOUND BY

LAST: Wilhite	FIRST: Carla	MIDDLE:

Kiowa Encampment Counselor

DATE FOUND: June 13th, 1977	TIME FOUND: 6am

BODIES FOUND IN OPEN AREA

SPECIFIC LOCATION: Trail near Kiowa encampment within the Camp Scott area

TYPE OF AREA: Wooded dirt trail

AREA CONDITION: DIRT, GRASS, WOODED AREA

NEAREST ROAD TO SCENE:	NAME OF ROAD:
DISTANCE FROM SCENE:	DIRECTION:

NEAREST POINT OF REFERENCE: Mayes County Electrical Pole

POSITION OF BODIES

POSITION: ON BACK, OTHER

DESCRIBE: 1 body on top a sleeping bag, 2 bodies inside sleeping bags

CONDITION OF BODY

BLOOD: PRESENT	IF PRESENT, LIST LOCATION: About the face

ANYTHING TIED TO BODY: YES

IF YES, DESCRIBE: Hands tied behind back, Type of gag around neck, Tape around hands and front of shirt.

LIGATURE MARKS: YES	IF YES, DESCRIBE. Ligature marks around neck

CLOTHING

CLOTHING: **PARTIALLY CLOTHED**
DESCRIBE CLOTHING: **Night shirt pulled up**

WOUNDS / WEAPONS

WOUNDS VISIBLE: **YES**	TYPE OF WOUND: **BLUNT FORCE**
MARKS ON BODY: **YES**	LOCATION OF MARKS / WOUNDS: **HEAD, NECK**

EVIDENCE OF SEXUAL BATTERY: **YES**
WEAPONS PRESENT: **NO**

EVIDENCE RECOVERED

EVIDENCE RECOVERED AT THE CRIME SCENE: **YES**

ITEMS COLLECTED AT THE CRIME SCENE

ITEMS PROCESSED FOR LATENT PRINTS: **YES**

ITEM	LOCATION
Partial roll of black tape	**Beside tree near bodies**
Red Flashlight	**Beside tree near bodies**
Glasses	**Near bodies on trail**
Glasses case	**Near bodies on trail**

TRACE EVIDENCE

BLOOD: **YES**	LOCATION: **Inside Victims tent**
HAIR: **YES**	LOCATION: **Inside Victims tent**
STAINS: **YES**	LOCATION: **Inside Victims tent**
TOOL MARKS: **YES**	LOCATION: **Inside Victims tent**

SHOE / TIRE TRACKS AND CASTING INFORMATION

SHOE TRACKS AT SCENE: **YES**
LOCATION / DESCRIBE: 2 shoeprints inside tent made from stepping in blood on wooden floor of tent, one size 10 military style boot, 2nd size 7 men's tennis shoe.

CASTING: **YES**	PHOTOGRAPHS: **YES**

TIRE TRACKS AT SCENE: **Unknown**
LOCATION / DESCRIBE: Barbara Day and husband observed car outside front camp gate night before – Sunday June 12th, 1977

151

WEATHER CONDITIONS IN TULSA OKLAHOMA ON JUNE 12 AND JUNE 13, 1977.

Time	Temp	Humidity	Visibility	Wind Dir	Wind Speed	Condition
June 12th, 1977						
5pm	94	41%	10.0 mi	WSW	5.8 mph	Mostly Cloudy
6pm	87	52%	0.5 mi	NNE	17.3 mph	Thunderstorm
7pm	82	67%	6.0 mi	NE	11.5 mph	Thunderstorm
8pm	80.1	71%	15.0 mi	SSE	11.5 mph	Rain
9pm	77	76%	15.0 mi	EAST	8.1 mph	Mostly Cloudy
10pm	75.9	79%	15.0 mi	SE	5.8 mph	Mostly Cloudy
11pm	75	82%	15.0 mi	EAST	4.6 mph	Overcast
June 13th, 1977						
12am	73.9	79%	15.0 mi	SSE	5.8 mph	Mostly Cloudy
1am	73	81%	15.0 mi	SSE	6.9 mph	Overcast
2am	72	87%	15.0 mi	EAST	5.8 mph	Overcast
3am	72	82%	15.0 mi	SOUTH	13.8 mph	Overcast
4am	72	87%	15.0 mi	SSW	8.1 mph	Overcast
5am	72	84%	15.0 mi	SW	4.6 mph	Mostly Cloudy
6am	71.1	87%	10 mi	SOUTH	4.6 mph	Mostly Cloudy

15

SOURCES

1 - *Frederick Daily Leader*, Frederick, OK, By UPI, June 15, 1977, Screams aroused Scouters, Pg 1

2 - *The Oklahoman*, By Debby Baxter, June 14, 1977, Mother's Wait Horrible, absolutely Horrible, Pg 1

3 - *The Oklahoman*, By Debby Baxter, June 14, 1977, Killings Frighten Nearby Town, Page 1

4 - *The Bryan Times*, By George W. Boosey, UPI, June 14, 1977, Close camp after murder of Girl Scouts, pg 9

5 - *Midweek*, The feature magazine of the Tulsa Tribune, By E.N. Earley, Investigation: The handling of the Girl Scouts' slaying case, Pg 1

6 - *The Daily Times*, Pryor, OK, By Ron Grimsley, June 16th, 1977, "Special dog team combs murder scene"

7 - *Midweek*, The feature magazine of the Tulsa Tribune, By E.N. Earley, Investigation: The handling of the Girl Scouts' slaying case, Page 1

8 - *Frederick Daily Leader*, Frederick, OK, By UPI, June 15, 1977, Memorial Funds Set Up For Trio Of Slain Girl Scouts, Pg 1&7

9 - *Frederick Daily Leader*, Frederick, OK, By UPI, June 15, 1977, Securities Increased At Youth Camps In Oklahoma, Pg 7

10 - *Midweek*, The feature magazine of the Tulsa Tribune, By E.N. Earley, Investigation: The handling of the Girl Scouts' slaying case, Pg 1

11- *Frederick Daily Leader*, By UPI, June 17, 1977, Search Dogs Roam Slaying Site Region, Pg 1

12 - *Tulsa World*, By Mary Hargrove, June 16, 1977, Few parents pull scouts out of camps

13 - *The Evening News*, Newburgh, New York, By AP News, June 16, 1977, Fingerprints Clues in Girl Scout Slayings, Pg 7B

14 - *Frederick Daily Leader*, By UPI, June 17, 1977, Burglaries Probed At Girl Scout Murder Site, Pg 1&6

15 - *Frederick Daily Leader*, By UPI, June 17, 1977, Slayer Can Confess On Special Hotline, Pg 1

16 - *Frederick Daily Leader*, By UPI, June 21, 1977, Guardsmen May Search Scout Murder Site, Page 1 & 6

17 - *Tulsa World*, By Rob Martindale, June 19, 1977, Evidence claimed in killings, page A-4

18 - *Frederick Daily Leader*, By UPI, June 19, 1977, Criminals, Not Camping, Dangerous To Citizens, Pg 1

19 - *Midweek*, The feature magazine of the Tulsa Tribune, By E.N. Earley, Investigation: The handling of the Girl Scouts' slaying case, Pg 1

20 - *Frederick Daily Leader*, By UPI, June 22, 1977, Guardsmen May Search Scout Murder Site, Pg 6

21 - *The Lawton Constitution*, AP, June 23, 1977, Slayings Suspect Named, Pg 1

22 - *Lawton Morning Press*, By AP News, Saturday, June 25, 1977, Farmer Who Saw Man In Cave Blames Self For Allowing Escape, page 9A

23 - *The Daily Times*, Pryor OK, By Ron Grimsley, June 26, 1977, Father remembers details of death on search of camp

24 - *Frederick Daily Leader*, By UPI, June 26, 1977, New 'Finds' In Slaying Of Scouts, Pg 1

25 - *Frederick Daily Leader*, By UPI, Hunt Goes On In Locust Grove Area, Pg 1

26 - *The Oklahoman*, By Ed Kelley, July 1, 1977, State Patrol Goes Home, Pg 79

27 - *Lawton Morning News*, AP, July 9th, 1977, Scout camp to reopen days only

28 - *The Daily Ardmoreite*, Ardmore Oklahoma, By Kay Evers, July 11, 1977, Expert Shows Mentality of Girls' Killer, Expects 'Repeat', page 1 and 2

29 - *Midweek*, The feature magazine of the Tulsa Tribune, By E.N. Earley, Investigation: The handling of the Girl Scouts' slaying case, Pg 1

30 - *The Tulsa Tribune*, By Jack Wimer, Shoes mysteriously appear at scout death scene, Pg 1

31 - *Ada Evening News*, By AP News, September 23, 1977

32 - *Frederick Daily Leader*, By UPI, September 23, 1977, Attach Dogs Donated To Camp Scott

33 - *The Southeast Missourian*, AP News, March 19, 1978, Murder Suspect is Wrong Man

34 - *Gadsden*, Alabama, By AP News, April 7, 1978, Police capture suspect in Scout murders, Pg 1

35 - *The Abilene Reporter-News*, Abilene, Texas, By AP News, April 12, 1978, Hart Pleads Innocent in Girl Scout Sex Slayings, Pg 1

36 - *The Bonham Daily Favorite*, By UPI, June 7, 1978, Hart Hearing Scheduled

37 - *Spokane Daily Chronicle*, By AP, June 7, 1978, Women Recalls Scout Death

38 - *Bangor Daily News*, By UPI, June 8, 1978, Girl Scout murders scene is described

39 - *The Bonham Daily Favorite*, By UPI, June 9, 1978, Note Warned Of Girl Scout Murders: Leader

40 - *The Spokesman Review*, By AP, June 9, 1978, Death warning found

41 - *The Bonham Daily Favorite*, Bonham, TX, By UPI, June 11, 1978, Prints Found In Scout Slayings, Pg 8

42 - *Williamson Daily News*, By AP, June 12, 1978, Preliminary trial still not linked Hart to killing of three Girl Scouts

43 - *The Deseret News*, Salt Lake City, Utah, By Vern Anderson, June 24, 1978, Security stepped up at Girl Scout camps, Pg 4A

44 - *The Bonham Daily Favorite*, By UPI, June 27, 1978, Girls Frightened By Men, Pg1

45 - *The Altus Times-Democrat*, By UPI, June 27, 1978, Unknown Men seen Near Scout Camp

46 - *The Bonham Daily Favorite*, By UPI, June 27, 1978, Girls Frightened By Men, Pg1

47 - *St. Joseph Gazette*, June 28, 1978, Testimony reveals tracks of 2 in slain girls' tent

48 - *The Altus Times-Democrat*, By UPI, June 28, 1978, Youth Saw Leroy Hart Near Scene of Slayings

49 - *The Tulsa Tribune*, By Tribune State Staff, June 30, 1978, 3 caves figure in Scout case

50 - *Tulsa World*, By Doug Hicks, Hart Ordered to stand Trial in 3 Sex Slayings

51 - *Tulsa Tribune*, By Susan Witt, November 24, 1978, Book was way to aid author, wise claimed

52 - *Frederick Daily Leader*, By UPI, March 4, 1979 – Leroy Hart Trial to begin Monday, Page 1

53 - *The Morning Record and Journal*, By UPI, March 20, 1979, Counselor testifies in Scout murders, Pg 10

54 - *The Alton Times-Democrat*, By UPI, March 22, 1979, Hart Jurors May Be Going to Campsite, Pg 7

55 - *Frederick Daily Leader*, By UPI, March 23, 1979, Hart Jury May See Camp Site, Pg 6

56 - *Frederick Daily Leader*, By UPI, March 27, 1979, Hair Discounted By Scientists In Hart's Trial, Pg 1 & 6

57 - *Frederick Daily Leader*, By UPI, March 29, 1979, Convict Suspected In Girl Scout Slayings, Pg 1 & 6

58 - *Tulsa World*, By Doug Hicks, March 31, 1979, Hart Innocent; Case Won't Be Reopened, Page 1

59 - *Tulsa Tribune*, By Tribune Wire Services, March 31, 1979, Hart Returned to Prison, Page 1A

60 - *The Oklahoman*, By AP News, April 19, 1979, Fellow Inmate Relates Stevens' Story of Killing Girl Scouts, OSBI Reports Say

C.S. Kelly

61 - *Tulsa Tribune*, By AP News, March 31, 1979, More damages asked, Families of slain Girl Scouts suing for $3.5 million

62 - *The Paper*, Pryor Creek Oklahoma, July 22, 2002, Pages 7 & 8, Interview with the Cherokee Advocate, By Cherokee National employees Jeff McLemore, Dan Garber and Gwenn LeMaster, The Hart interview

63 - *The Daily Oklahoman*, By Griff Palmer, March 31, 1985, Hart Legacy One of State's Nagging Murder Mysteries, http://newsok.com/hart-legacy-one-of-states-nagging-murder-mysteries/article/2103521

64 - *The Oklahoman*, By Judy Fossett, June 13, 1979, Kansas Links Probed in Girl Scout Incidents, Page 102

65 - *World Tribune*, August 8, 1980, Ex-OSBI Agent Brothers Sell Book About Girl Scout Killings

66 - *Tulsa World*, By Brian Barber World Staff Writer, June 9, 1997, Updated 5/25/08, Murders Put Council, Families in Different Worlds, http://www.tulsaworld.com/article.aspx/Murders_Put_Council_Families_in_Different_Worlds/19970608_Ne_focus2

67 - *The Oklahoman*, By Don Hayden, Staff Writer, June 13, 1982, Future of Camp Scott Remains in Doubt, page 230

68 - *The Daily Oklahoman*, By Robby Trammell, May 12, 1984, 3 Investigated in Scout Slayings, http://newsok.com/3-investigated-in-scout-slayings/article/2067916

69 - *The Daily Oklahoman*, By Robby Trammell, May 16, 1984, OSBI Discounts "New' Scout Slaying Information, http://newsok.com/osbi-discounts-new-scout-slaying-information/article/2068357

70 - *The Daily Oklahoman*, June 17, 1984, Slain Scout's Parents Form Group, http://newsok.com/slain-scouts-parents-form-group/article/2071850

71 - *The Daily Oklahoman*, By Robby Trammell, June 13, 1984, Sheriff Vows to Continue Girl Scout Murder Investigation, http://newsok.com/sheriff-vows-to-continue-girl-scout-murder-investigation/article/2071363

72 - *The Daily Oklahoman*, By Judy Fossett, July 16, 1984, Answers to Scout Murders Case Gone With Slain Former Suspect, Pg 85

73 - *The Daily Oklahoman*, By Griff Palmer, March 19, 1985 Trial of Suit Involving 1977 Scout Slayings Starts, http://newsok.com/trial-of-suit-involving-1977-scout-slayings-starts/article/2102152

74 - *The Daily Oklahoman*, March 28, 1985, by Griff Palmer, Jury Finds in Favor Of Scout Council Slain Girls' Parents "Shocked', http://newsok.com/jury-finds-in-favor-of-scout-council-slain-girls-parents-shocked/article/2103189

75 - *The Daily Oklahoman*, By Griff Palmer, March 29, 1985, Sheriff Checking "Lead" in Scout slayings, http://newsok.com/sheriff-checking-lead-in-girl-scout-slayings/article/2103289

76 - *The Daily Oklahoman*, June 7, 1985, Parents of 2 Slain Girls File Appeal, http://newsok.com/parents-of-2-slain-girls-file-appeal/article/2111129

77 - *The Daily Oklahoman*, By Chris Casteel, December 17, 1986, Scouts Ruled Not Liable In 3 Murders http://newsok.com/scouts-ruled-not-liable-in-3-murders/article/2169354

78 - *The Daily Oklahoman*, August 29, 1988, Scout Board Selling Site of Campers' Unsolved Murders, http://newsok.com/scout-board-selling-site-of-campers-unsolved-murders/article/2237339

79 - *Tulsa World*, Ken Jackson, June 11th, 1989, Wanna Start Something? Start Asking Why Book Was Pulled, http://www.tulsaworld.com/article.aspx/Wanna_Start_Something_Start_Asking_Why_Book_Was_Pulled/38672

80 - *Tulsa World*, By Randy Pruitt, July 26, 1989, FBI Trying to Solve Girl Scout Murders With DNA, http://www.tulsaworld.com/article.aspx/FBI_Trying_to_Solve_Girl _Scout_Murders_With_DNA/51295

81 - *Tulsa World*, by Joe Stumpe, October 24, 1989, DNA tests fail to solve Girl Scout killings, http://www.tulsaworld.com/article.aspx/DNA_tests_fail_to_solve _Girl_Scout_killings/75247

82 - *The Daily Oklahoman*, By Robby Trammell, October 25, 1989, DNA Tests Link Gene Leroy Hart to Girl Scout Deaths, http://newsok.com/dna-tests-link-gene-leroy-hart-to-girl-scout-deaths/article/2287953) Also (Tulsa World, By Jim Myers, October 25, 1989, Updated 8/20/08, Lid Kept on DNA Results in Girl Scout Killings, http://www.tulsaworld.com/article.aspx/Lid_Kept_on_DNA_Results_in_Girl_Scout_Killings/75657

83 - *Tulsa World*, By Melinda Morris, August 20, 1990, Minister claims he saw killers in '77 Camp Scott murder case, http://www.tulsaworld.com/article.aspx/Minister _claims_he_saw_killers_in_77_Camp_Scott_murder/152185

84 - *Tulsa World*, By Emily D. Slier, November 21, 1990, No New Light Shed on Scout Murders, http://www.tulsaworld.com/article.aspx/No_New_Light_Shed_on_Scout _Murders/176443

85 - *The Daily Oklahoman*, By AP News, October 13, 1991, Ex-Sheriff Who Investigated Girl Scout Killings Dies at 71, http://newsok.com/ex-sheriff-who-investigated-girl-scout-killings-dies-at-71/article/2371929

86 - *Tulsa World*, By Tony Lee Orr, March 23, 1993, Suit Seeks Items Claimed as Girl Scout Slayings Link, http://www.tulsaworld.com/article.aspx/Suit_Seeks_Items _Claimed _as_Girl_Scout_Slayings_Link/380457

87 - *Tulsa World*, June 2nd, State-area deaths, http://www.tulsaworld.com/article.aspx/STATE_AREA_DEATHS/391769

88 - *The Daily Oklahoman*, By AP News, October 2, 1994, Ex-Agent Now Filmmaker Details State Girl Scout Murders of '77, page 10, http://newsok.com/ex-agent-now-filmmaker-details-state-girl-scout-murders-of-77/article/2479433

89 - *The Daily Oklahoman*, By AP News, June 8, 1996, Petition Seeks New Look at 1977 Girl Scout Murders, http://newsok.com/petition-seeks-new-look-at-1977-girl-scout-murders/article/2543194

90 - *Tulsa World*, By AP News, June 11, 1996, Judge Nixes Scout Murder Case Petition, http://www.tulsaworld.com/article.aspx/Judge_Nixes_Scout_Murder_Case_Petition/570554

C.S. Kelly

91 - *Tulsa World*, By AP News, June 13, 1996, Man Not Giving Up on Grand Jury Petition, http://www.tulsaworld.com/article.aspx/Man_Not_Giving_Up_on_Grand_Jury_Petition/570838

92 - *Tulsa World*, By Linda Martin, June 15, 1996, Court OK's Petition in Girl Scout Case, http://www.tulsaworld.com/article.aspx/Court_OKs_Petition_In_Girl_Scout_Case/571156

93 - *Tulsa World*, By Linda Martin, July 4, 1996, Triple Murder Probe Delayed, http://www.tulsaworld.com/article.aspx/Triple_Murder_Probe_Delayed/573834

94 - *Tulsa World*, By Linda Martin, November 16, 1996, New Probe Sought in 1977 Girl Scout Murders, http://www.tulsaworld.com/article.aspx/New_Probe_Sought_in_1977_Girl_Scout_Murders/593002

95 - *Tulsa World*, By Linda Martin, November 20, 1996, Grand Jury Petition in Scout Deaths OK'd, http://www.tulsaworld.com/article.aspx/Grand_Jury_Petition_In_Scout_Deaths_OKd/19961119_Ne_a7grand

96 - *The Daily Oklahoman*, By Mark A. Hutchison, December 25, 1996 – Law Toughens Petition Task 2nd Bid Launched for Grand Jury on Deaths, http://newsok.com/law-toughens-petition-task-2nd-bid-launched-for-grand-jury-on-deaths/article/2559676

97 - *Tulsa World*, By AP Wire Service, January 22nd, 1997, Judge: Girl Scout Case Won't Be Reopened, http://www.tulsaworld.com/article.aspx/Judge_Girl_Scout_Case_Wont_Be_Reopened/19970121_Ne_a12judge

98 - *Tulsa World*, February 25, 1997, Retired Police Officer Dies, http://www.tulsaworld.com/article.aspx/Retired_Police_Officer_Dies/606505

99 - *Tulsa World*, By Pam Olson, May 19, 2002, DNA tests fail in 1977 murders, http://www.tulsaworld.com/article.aspx/DNA_tests_fail_in_1977_murders/020518_Ne_a13dnate

100 - *The Paper*, Pryor Creek, Oklahoma, By Terry Aylward, July 8, 2002, Up against the wall, Page 7

101 - The Paper, Pryor Creek, Oklahoma, By Terry Aylward, July 8, 2002, Counties wanted grand jury in 1996, Page 9

102 - *The Paper*, Pryor Creek, Oklahoma, By Terry Aylward, June 10, 2002, Evidence still being held here, Page 9

103 – *OETA*, By Susan Miller,October 2003, Missing Pieces, Oklahoma Girl Scout Murders, http://www.oeta.tv/stateline/transcripts/618-502-qmissing-piecesq.html

104 - *Tulsa World*, By Rhett Morgan, May 25, 2007, Area officials watching new DNA test closely, http://www.tulsaworld.com/article.aspx/Area_officials_watching_new_DNA_test_closely/070525_1_A8_ANWor56181 *Tulsa World*, By AP Wire Service, September 9, 2007, Second DNA set in 1977 murders, http://www.tulsaworld.com/article.aspx/Second_DNA_set_in_1977_murders/070909_1_A20_spanc77621

105 - *The Oklahoman*, By Ron Jackson, June 25, 2008, Was a female involved in 1977 Girl Scout slayings?, http://newsok.com/was-a-female-involved-in-1977-girl-scout-slayings/article/3261879/?tm=1214395135 & *NewsOn6.com*, By AP News, June24, 2008 , DNA Testing Inconclusive In Girl Scout Murder Case, http: //www.Newson 6. com/story/8545813/dna-testing-inconclusive-in-girl-scout-murder-case

106 - *Tulsa World*, By Tim Stanley, Mar 24, 2010, Beloved Girl Scouts leader taught camp skills, life lessons, http://www.tulsaworld.com/article.aspx/Beloved_Girl_Scouts_leader_taught_camp_skills_life/20100324_11_a11_anacco495753 & *The Daily Oklahoman*, By Griff Palmer, March 27, 1985, Camp Director Denies Counselors' Warnings, http://newsok.com/camp-director-denies-counselors-warnings/article/2103069

107 - *The Times*, Pryor Creek, Oklahoma, By Melissa McClendon, June 13, 2011, New book revisits Girl Scout Murders, http://pryordailytimes.com/features/x1943989959/New-book-revisits-Girl-Scout-Murders

108 - *ABCNEWS.COM*, By RESHMA KIRPALANI, June 8, 2011, Ex-Con Claims His Film Will Solve Case, http://abcnews.go.com/US/1977-girl-scout-murders-con-claims-film-solve/story?id=14022194

109 - *Tulsa World*, By Michael Smith, World Scene Writer, July 12, 2011, National media spotlights Girl Scout murder case,http://www.tulsaworld.com/site/printerfriendl ystory.aspx?articleid=20110712_283_D6_Fourwe353876

110 - *Tulsa World*, By Tim Stanley, World Staff Writer, January 13, 2012 Former Rogers County prosecutor dies, http://www.tulsaworld.com/article.aspx/Former_Rogers_County_prosecutor_dies/20120113_11_a15_ulnsbe884519

111 - *NewsOn6.com*, By Russell Hulstine, December 31, 2012, Man convicted of Broken Arrow Murder dies in Prison, http://www.newson6.com/story/20473989/rogers-county-convicted-murder-dies-in-state-prison

112 - *The Oklahoman*, Tim Farley, June 26, 1988, Families Cope With Death of Children, http://newsok.com/families-cope-with-death-of-children/article/2230448

113 - *The Paper*, Pryor Creek, Oklahoma, June 24, 2002, Remembering Michele, Pg 8

114 - *The Daily Oklahoman*, Griff Palmer, March 23, 1985, Slain Scout's Dad Testifies at Suit Trial, Recalls Girl's Exceptional Memory, http://newsok.com/slain-scouts-dad-testifies-at-suit-trial-recalls-girls-exceptional-memory/article/2102654

115 - *The Paper*, Pryor Creek, Oklahoma, June 17, 2002, Remembering Lori, Pg 8

116 - *Tulsa World*, By Brian Barber, June 9, 1997, Elusive Truth, http://www.tulsaworld.com/article.aspx/Elusive_Truth/19970608_Ne_focus1

117 - *The Daily Oklahoman*, Griff Palmer, March 23, 1985, Slain Scout's Dad Testifies at Suit Trial, Recalls Girl's Exceptional Memory, http://newsok.com/slain-scouts-dad-testifies-at-suit-trial-recalls-girls-exceptional-memory/article/2102654

118 - *Tulsa People*, A MEMOIR BY HARVEY BLUMENTHAL, The Tulsa Life and Times of Ralph and Jack and Me, http://www.tulsapeople.com/Tulsa-People/December-2012/The-Tulsa-Life-and-Times-of-Ralph-and-Jack-and-Me/index.php?cparticle=1&siarticle=0#artanc

119 - *The Oklahoman*, By Charles T. Jones, June 10, 1997, Modified June 22, 2007, Girl Scout Murders Still Touching Lives Two Decades Later, http://newsok.com/girl-scout-killings-still-touching-lives-2-decades-later/article/2583679) (The Tulsa Tribune, By Steve Ward, June 5,1987, Aftermath, Girl Scouts slain 10 years ago, Pg 1&4

120 - *The Paper*, Pryor Creek, Oklahoma, By Terry Aylward, July 10, 2002, The Crime That Shocked The Nation

121 - *The Daily Oklahoman*, Griff Palmer, March 23, 1985, Slain Scout's Dad Testifies at Suit Trial, Recalls Girl's Exceptional Memory, http://newsok.com/slain-scouts-dad-testifies-at-suit-trial-recalls-girls-exceptional-memory/article/2102654

122 - *The Bonham Daily Favorite*, By UPI, June 17, 1977, Slain Girl's Service, Pg 1

123 - *Tulsa World*, February 25, 1997, Retired Police Officer Dies, http://www.tulsaworld.com/article.aspx/Retired_Police_Officer_Dies/606505
124 - *The Paper*, Pryor Creek, Oklahoma, June 10, 2002, The Crime That Shocked The Nation, Pg 7)(The Paper, Pryor Creek, Oklahoma, June 24th, 2002, Thousands attended camp Scott before, Pg 10

125 - *Frederick Daily Leader*, By UPI, December 6, 1977, Camp Scott Redesigned, http://news.google.com/newspapers?id=0VRDAAAAIBAJ&sjid=mK0MAAAAIBAJ&pg=3378,5241459&dq=ginny+young+magic+empire+council&hl=en, Pg 4
126 - *The Daily Oklahoman*, By Don Hayden, June 13, 1982, Future of Camp Scott Remains in Doubt, Girl Scout Reservation Has Never Reopened Since Slayings

127 - *The Daily Oklahoman*, By AP News, August 29, 1988, Scout Board Selling Site of Campers' Unsolved Murders

128 - *The Tulsa Tribune*, By Steve Ward, June 5, 1987, Aftermath, Girl Scouts slain 10 years ago, Pg 1&4

129 - *Frederick Daily Leader*, By UPI, June 17, 1977, Scout Slaying Similar To Death 14 Years Ago, Pg 6

130 - *The Altus Times Democrat*, By UPI, June 27, 1978, Unknown Men seen Near Scout Camp

131 - *The Evening News*, Newburgh, New York, By AP News, June 16,1977, Fingerprints Clues in Girl Scout Slayings, Pg 7B

132 – *Frederick Daily Leader*, By UPI, July 31, 1977, Victims Shoes Add Strange New Twist In Scout Killings, Pg 1

133 - *Frederick Daily Leader*, By UPI, June 29, 1977, Girl Scout Drug From Tent In Sarasota, Fla., Pg 1

134 - *Frederick Daily Leader*, By UPI, June 30, 1977, No Further Word Heard From Abducted Girl, 15, Pg 6

135 - *Frederick Daily Leader*, By UPI, July 3, 1977, Florida Girl Scout Released, Pg 1

136 *The Daily Oklahoman*, By Griff Palmer, March 19, 1985, Trial of Suit Involving 1977 Scout Slayings Starts, http://newsok.com/trial-of-suit-involving-1977-scout-slayings-starts/article/2102152

137 - *The Daily Oklahoman*, Griff Palmer, March 20, 1985, Parents of Slain Scouts Claim Camp Poorly Operated, http://newsok.com/parents-of-slain-scouts-claim-camp-poorly-operated/article/2102241

138 - *The Daily Oklahoman*, Griff Palmer, March 21, 1985, Survivor Didn't Like Tent Where Girls Died, http://newsok.com/survivor-didnt-like-tent-where-girls-died/article/2102373

139 - *The Daily Oklahoman*, Griff Palmer, March 22, 1985, Scout Camp Security Plan Questioned, http://newsok.com/scout-camp-security-plan-questioned/article/2102476
140 - *The Daily Oklahoman*, Griff Palmer, March 26, 1985, Camp Workers Testify No Warning of Danger, http://newsok.com/camp-workers-testify-no-warning-of-danger/article/2102967

141 - *The Daily Oklahoman*, Griff Palmer, March 27, 1985, Camp Director Denies Counselors' Warnings, http://newsok.com/camp-director-denies-counselors-warnings/article/2103069

142 - *The Daily Oklahoman*, Griff Palmer, March 28, 1985, Jury Finds in Favor of Scout Council Slain Girls Parents shocker, http://newsok.com/jury-finds-in-favor-of-scout-council-slain-girls-parents-shocked/article/2103189

143 - *The Oklahoman*, By AP News, June 7, 1985, Parents of 2 Slain Girls File Appeal, Pg 31

144 - *Tulsa World*, By Randy Pruitt & Samuel Autman, July 26th, 1989, FBI Trying to Solve Girl Scout Murders With DNA, Pg 1

145 - *The Daily Oklahoman*, By AP, August 2, 1989, FBI Recommends California Lab For Old Evidence, http://newsok.com/fbi-recommends-california-lab-for-old-evidence/article/2274745

146 - *Tulsa World*, Lid Kept on DNA Results in Girl Scout Killings, By Jim Myers on Oct 25, 1989, updated 8/20/08, http://www.tulsaworld.com/article.aspx/Lid_Kept_on_DNA_Results_in_Girl_Scout_Killings/75657

147 - *Tulsa World*, By PAM OLSON World Correspondent, May 19, 2002, DNA tests fail in 1977 murders, http://www.tulsaworld.com/article.aspx/DNA_tests_fail_in_1977_murders/020518_Ne_a13dnate

148 – *The Oklahoman*, June 25, 2008 DNA tests bring more questions Was a female involved in 1977 Girl Scout slayings? & NewsOn6.com, June 24, 2008, DNA Testing Inconclusive In Girl Scout Murder Case and *Claremore Daily Progress*, July 15, 2008

149 - *Cedar Rapids Gazette*, AP News, March 30, 1980, Girl Scout slayings still a mystery

150 - *The Daily Oklahoman*, By Randy Ellis, Modified: June 13, 1982, Published: June 13, 1982, Girl Scout Slayings 5 Years Ago Still Haunt Families, http://newsok.com/girl-scout-slayings-5-years-ago-still-haunt-families/article/1986754

151 - *The Daily Oklahoman*, by Tim Farley, Modified: June 26, 1988, Published: June 26, 1988, Families Cope with Death of Children, http://newsok.com/families-cope-with-death-of-children/article/2230448

152 - *Tulsa World*, By Brian Barber on Jun 9, 1997, updated on 5/25/08, Murders put Council, Families in Different worlds, http://www.tulsaworld.com/article.aspx/Murders_Put_Council_Families_in_Different_Worlds/620534

C.S. Kelly

153 - *Tulsa World*, By Brian Barber on Jun 9, 1997, Updated on 5/25/08, 20 Years Later, Slaying at Camp Still Shock, Horrify, http://www.tulsaworld.com/article.aspx/20_Years_Later_Slayings_at_Camp_Still_Shock_Horrify/620163

154 - *Tulsa World*, BY Brian Barber, Jun 9, 1997, 5/25/08 at 2:00 AM, Elusive Truth // Speculation Still Rampant 20 Years After Slayings, http://www.tulsaworld.com/site/printerfriendlystory.aspx?articleid=620535

155 - *Tulsa World*, By PAM OLSON World Correspondent, Jun 9, 2002, Shadow of doubt, http://www.tulsaworld.com/site/printerfriendlystory.aspx?articleid=020609_Ne_a1unset

156 - *The Daily Oklahoman*, By Melissa Merideth, Rebecca Lange, Modified: June 22, 2007 at 2:23 pm, Published: June 13, 2002, Girl Scout Killings Still Haunt State

157 - *Tulsa World*, BY DAVID HARPER World Staff Writer, Wednesday, June 13, 2007, http://www.tulsaworld.com/site/printerfriendlystory.aspx?articleid=070613_1_A1_spanc46170

158 - *The Oklahoman*, By Ron Jackson, Modified: July 18, 2007 at 5:21 pm, Published: June 17, 2007, 1977 killings changed the face of security at summer, http://newsok.com/1977-killings-changed-the-face-of-security-at-summer-camps/article/3067125

159 - *Tulsa World*, June 26th, 2008, By World's Editorial Writers, No DNA clues – Link not found in Scout murders, http://www.tulsaworld.com/site/printerfriendlystory.aspx? articleid=20080626_61_A12_hEDITO245585

160 – *Someone Cry For The Children*, 1981, By Michael Wilkerson and Dick Wilkerson, Publisher: Dial Press, ISBN-10: 0803782837

161 - *The Oklahoman*, Murder case's lore, mystery keep growing, By Ron Jackson, June 29, 2008, http://newsok.com/murder-cases-lore-mystery-keep growing/article/3263505

162 – *The Oklahoman*, May 7, 1985, New Trial Plea Rejected in Lawsuit Against Girl Scout Council, Page 40

163 - *Oklahoma State Bureau of Investigation*, March 7, 2014, OSBI Continues Work on Decades-Old Girl Scouts Murder Case, http://www.ok.gov/osbi/Press_Room/2014_Press_Releases/PR-2014-03-07__OSBI_CONTINUES_WORK_ON_DECADES_OLD_GIRL_SCOUTS_MURDER_CASE.html

164 – ODCR, *State of Oklahoma vs. Hart, Gene*, Transcript of Preliminary Hearing, Volume I, CRF-77-131, 132 & 133, http://www1.odcr.com/detail?court=049-&casekey=049-CRF+7700131

165 – ODCR, *State of Oklahoma vs. Hart, Gene*, Transcript of Preliminary Hearing, Volume II, CRF-77-131, 132 & 133, http://www1.odcr.com/detail?court=049-&casekey=049-CRF+7700131

166 – ODCR, *State of Oklahoma vs. Hart, Gene*, Transcript of Preliminary Hearing, Volume III, CRF-77-131, 132 & 133, http://www1.odcr.com/detail?court=049-&casekey=049-CRF+7700131

167 – ODCR, *State of Oklahoma vs. Hart, Gene,* Transcript of Preliminary Hearing, Volume IV, CRF-77-131, 132 & 133, http://www1.odcr.com/detail?court=049-&casekey=049-CRF+7700131

168 – ODCR, *State of Oklahoma vs. Hart, Gene,* Transcript of Preliminary Hearing, Volume V, CRF-77-131, 132 & 133, http://www1.odcr.com/detail?court=049-&casekey=049-CRF+7700131

169 – ODCR, *State of Oklahoma vs. Hart, Gene,* Transcript of Preliminary Hearing, Volume VI, CRF-77-131, 132 & 133, http://www1.odcr.com/detail?court=049-&casekey=049-CRF+7700131

170 – ODCR, *State of Oklahoma vs. Hart, Gene,* Transcript of Preliminary Hearing, Volume VII, CRF-77-131, 132 & 133, http://www1.odcr.com/detail?court=049-&casekey=049-CRF+7700131

171 – ODCR, *State of Oklahoma vs. Hart, Gene,* Transcript of Preliminary Hearing, Volume VIII, CRF-77-131, 132 & 133, http://www1.odcr.com/detail?court=049-&casekey=049-CRF+7700131

172 – ODCR, *State of Oklahoma vs. Hart, Gene,* Transcript of Preliminary Hearing, Volume IX, CRF-77-131, 132 & 133, http://www1.odcr.com/detail?court=049-&casekey=049-CRF+7700131

173 – ODCR, *State of Oklahoma vs. Hart, Gene,* Transcript of Preliminary Hearing, Volume X, CRF-77-131, 132 & 133, http://www1.odcr.com/detail?court=049-&casekey=049-CRF+7700131

174 – ODCR, *State of Oklahoma vs. Hart, Gene,* Transcript of Preliminary Hearing, Volume XI, CRF-77-131, 132 & 133, http://www1.odcr.com/detail?court=049-&casekey=049-CRF+7700131

175 – ODCR, *State of Oklahoma vs. Hart, Gene,* Transcript of Preliminary Hearing, Volume XII, CRF-77-131, 132 & 133, http://www1.odcr.com/detail?court=049-&casekey=049-CRF+7700131

176 – ODCR, *State of Oklahoma vs. Hart, Gene,* Transcript of Preliminary Hearing, Volume XIII, CRF-77-131, 132 & 133, http://www1.odcr.com/detail?court=049-&casekey=049-CRF+7700131

Made in the USA
Coppell, TX
04 June 2021